Learning English

Grammar in Profile

Exercises for Upper Level

Teacher's Book

von Rosemary Hellyer-Jones

Ernst Klett Verlag
Stuttgart Düsseldorf Leipzig

Learning English
Grammar in Profile
Exercises for Upper Level

Teacher's Book von Rosemary Hellyer-Jones M.A., Ehingen (Donau)

Inhalt

Vorwort 3	12 Gerunds 37
1 Present Tense – Simple and Progressive . . . 4	13 Participles 39
2 Past Tense – Simple and Progressive 7	14 Non-finite Verb Forms: Mixed Exercises 42
3 Present Perfect – Simple and Progressive . . 10	15 Verbs and their Objects 45
4 Past Tense and Present Perfect Contrasted . 12	16 Relative Clauses 48
5 Forms of the Future 15	17 The Use of Adjectives and Adverbs 51
6 Sequence of Tenses 17	18 Adjectives and Adverbs:
7 Conditional Sentences 20	Comparative and Superlative Forms 53
8 Reported Speech 24	19 The Position of Adverbs and Adverbials 55
9 The Passive Voice 28	20 The Definite and the Indefinite Article 58
10 Modal Auxiliaries 31	21 Indefinite Pronouns and Determines 61
11 The Infinitive 34	22 Reflexive and Reciprocal Pronouns 62

Gedruckt auf Recyclingpapier,
hergestellt aus 100% Altpapier.

1. Auflage   1 10 9 8 7 6 | 2004 2003 2002 2001 2000

Alle Drucke dieser Auflage können im Unterricht nebeneinander benutzt werden, sie sind untereinander unverändert.
Die letzte Zahl bezeichnet das Jahr dieses Druckes.
© Ernst Klett Verlag GmbH, Stuttgart 1991. Alle Rechte vorbehalten.
Internetadresse: http://www.klett-verlag.de

Redaktion: Inge Schäfer, Verlagsredakteurin

Satz: Lihs GmbH, Medienhaus, Ludwigsburg.
Druck: Druckhaus Vogel, Echterdingen
ISBN 3-12-506250-0

Vorwort

Das vorliegende Lehrerbuch zu *Grammar in Profile* soll die Unterrichtsvorbereitung erleichtern, indem es Lösungen oder – bei Aufgaben, die unterschiedliche Formulierungen zulassen – Lösungsbeispiele zu den *Basic* und *Advanced Exercises* liefert. (Der Schlüssel zu den *Check-up*-Übungen ist bereits im Schülerbuch enthalten.) Lediglich bei Fragen nach persönlichen Meinungen und Erfahrungen werden keine Musterlösungen angeboten, da die Antworten nicht vorhersehbar sind. Da alle Aufgaben, auch solche, die unterschiedlich beantwortet werden können, auf die Verwendung bestimmter Strukturen abzielen und oft auch explizit dazu auffordern, sind diese Strukturen in den Lösungsvorschlägen durch Fettdruck hervorgehoben.

Darüber hinaus enthält das Lehrerbuch eine Reihe von Hintergrundinformationen, die für Lehrer und Schüler interessant sein könnten, darunter vor allem biographische Angaben zu den Autoren der authentischen Texte *(Notes on the authors)*. Außerdem wird durch in die Lösungen integrierte *Notes* auf Besonderheiten bei der Verwendung bestimmter Strukturen im jeweiligen Text hingewiesen, die nicht in den *Basic* oder *Advanced Rules* behandelt werden und die Anlaß zu Fragen geben könnten. (Die Abkürzungen GG und GhE beziehen sich, wie im Schülerbuch, auf die *Grundgrammatik* und die *Grammatik des heutigen Englisch*.)

Da die Übungsziele deutlich aus den Aufgabenstellungen hervorgehen, wurde auf Lernzielangaben verzichtet.

Die Übungsformen in *Grammar in Profile* sind vielfältig und erlauben methodisch abwechslungsreiche Verfahren: schriftliche oder mündliche Bearbeitung, Einzel-, Partner- und Gruppenarbeit oder eine gemeinsame Erarbeitung im Unterrrichtsgespräch. Welches Vorgehen sich jeweils empfiehlt, hängt nicht nur von der Aufgabe selbst ab, sondern auch von den individuellen Gegebenheiten wie Klassen- bzw. Kurszusammensetzung und Unterrichtssituation. Deshalb wird auf die methodischen Hinweise zu jeder einzelnen Aufgabe verzichtet. Statt dessen sollen hier nur ein paar allgemeine Vorschläge zur Behandlung der häufigsten Übungsformen gemacht werden, die auch auf deren Abwandlungen übertragen werden können und die zu individuellen methodischen Varianten anregen könnten.

Arbeit mit Originaltexten:
Bevor die Fragen beantwortet werden, sollte der Text aufmerksam gelesen und verstanden worden sein. Dies kann entweder als Stillesephase im Unterricht oder als häusliche Vorbereitung geschehen.

Die erste Aufgabe ist meist eine Aufforderung, die in den *Basic* oder *Advanced Rules* vorgestellten Strukturen im Text aufzusuchen. Am ökonomischsten ist es, wenn die Schüler zunächst die betreffenden Strukturen im Text unterstreichen. (Bei Leihbüchern sollte dies ganz leicht mit einem weichen Bleistift geschehen, so daß die Linien hinterher spurenlos ausradiert werden können.) Für unterschiedliche Strukturen können unterschiedliche Arten der Unterstreichung verwendet werden (einfach, doppelt, gestrichelt usw.). Anschließend wird jede Struktur besprochen und anhand der *Basic Rules* erklärt. Bei längeren Textpassagen kann die Arbeit auf mehrere Gruppen verteilt werden. Entweder übernimmt jede Gruppe einen anderen Abschnitt, oder jede Gruppe sucht innerhalb des ganzen Textes nach einer anderen Struktur. In Kapitel 14, *Advanced Exercise 2*, Frage 1 sollen z. B. alle infiniten Konstruktionen gefunden werden. Hier könnte eine Gruppe alle Infinitive, eine zweite alle *gerunds* und die dritte und vierte alle *present* bzw. *past participles* suchen.

Die anderen textbezogenen Aufgaben eignen sich meist ebenfalls zur mündlichen Bearbeitung, wobei den Schülern ggf. Zeit zur nochmaligen Lektüre des Textes oder bestimmter Passagen eingeräumt werden sollte.

Einsetz- und andere Übungen mit eindeutigen Lösungen:
In den meisten Fällen empfiehlt sich eine zeitsparende mündliche Bearbeitung. Dies gilt vor allem für Lückentexte, wenn das einzusetzende Wort zu jeder Lücke fest vorgegeben ist und nur über die richtige Form entschieden werden muß (z. B. Kapitel 1, *Basis Exercise 2*) oder wenn es für jede Lücke nur eine begrenzte, überschaubare Anzahl von Alternativen gibt (z. B. Kapitel 20, *Basic Exercise 2*; Kapitel 21, *Basic Exercise 2*). Auch Umformungsübungen (z. B. Kapitel 13, *Basic Exercise 4*) können in der Regel leicht mündlich bearbeitet werden.

Lückentexte, bei denen die einzusetzenden Wörter nicht chronologisch, sondern alphabetisch vorgege-

1 Present Tense – Simple and Progressive

ben werden (z. B. Kapitel 13, *Basic Exercise 2*) sowie Übungen, bei denen eine größere Zahl von Teilsätzen einander richtig zugeordnet werden müssen (z. B. Kapitel 7, *Advanced Exercise 1*) sind dagegen meist ‚Knobelaufgaben', deren Lösung zumindest schriftliche Notizen erfordert. Hier könnte es sich empfehlen, zur raschen Korrektur eine Folie mit den Lösungen vorzubereiten.

Übersetzungen:
Sowohl bei Hin- als auch bei Herübersetzungen empfiehlt sich zunächst eine schriftliche Lösung in Einzel- oder Gruppenarbeit. Anschließend werden die Ergebnisse besprochen und miteinander verglichen. Dabei einigt man sich auf eine gemeinsame Musterübersetzung, die ggf. an der Tafel oder auf einer Folie festgehalten wird.

Bildgesteuerte Übungen:
Auch hier empfiehlt sich eine schriftliche Bearbeitung, eventuell in Gruppen, wobei die verschiedenen Lösungsvorschläge anschließend vorgetragen und gemeinsam besprochen werden.

Freie Meinungsäußerung und Erfahrungsaustausch:
Fragen, die zu diesen Tätigkeiten auffordern, sollten mündlich beantwortet werden und führen im Idealfall zu einer lebhaften Diskussion. Dabei sollten die Schüler bewußt zur wiederholten Verwendung der jeweils zu übenden Strukturen angeleitet werden. Zur Steuerung können Diskussionsanstöße und entsprechende Redemittel an der Tafel oder auf Folie vorgegeben werden.

Andere offene Übungen:
Zwischen den Übungen mit eindeutigen Lösungen und den Aufforderungen zum freien Ausdruck persönlicher Meinungen und Erfahrungen liegt ein breites Spektrum von Mischformen mit unterschiedlichem Ausmaß der formalen und inhaltlichen Steuerung. Übersetzungen und bildgesteuerte Übungen wurden bereits erwähnt. Bei anderen offenen Übungsformen empfehlen wir als Faustregel eine schriftliche Erarbeitung, wenn die Formulierung längerer zusammenhängender Texte verlangt wird, und eine mündliche Beantwortung bei kürzeren Äußerungen.

1 Present Tense – Simple and Progressive

Basic Exercises

1 What's the moral?

1 *Picture 1:* A woman **is sitting** on the sofa surrounded by her dogs. Two of them **are lying** next to her, two others **are lying** on the floor, and the fifth **is climbing/wants** to climb (up) onto her knee. She **is dreaming** of another dog – an even bigger one (an Alsatian/a German Shepherd) – to join the others.
Picture 2: It **is** Valentine's Day. A girl **is sitting** at her desk, but she **isn't working**. She **is looking** at the three Valentine cards she has received. She **is thinking** about who may have sent them. She obviously **feels** very happy.
Picture 3: It **is** Father's birthday. He **is opening** his presents. He **looks** rather surprised because his wife and daughter have both given him the same thing – a recipe book. The wife and daughter **are smiling** at each other/**are laughing/are looking** at each other in amusement, because they have both had the same idea.
Picture 4: Mother and Father **are doing** the spring cleaning. Mother **is putting** up the freshly washed curtains, and Father **is vaccuuming/cleaning** the sofa. Their little child **is helping**. He/She **is emptying/pouring** a bucketful of water onto a house plant. Most of the water **is running** onto the carpet.
Picture 5: It **is** 9 o'clock on the first day of the Sales/sale. Lots of women **are rushing** to the door of a big clothes shop/department store, and the manager/one of the assistants **is** just **opening** the doors.
Picture 6: A woman/businesswoman **is lying** in bed. She **is trying** to sleep but can't, because she **is worrying** so much about all the things she **has** to do. She **is thinking** about her appointments and travelling arrangements/travel plans, her work at the office, and – on top of it all – the work she still **has** to do in the garden.

2 *Picture 1:* The more you **get**, the more you **want**.
Picture 2: It's love that **makes** the world go round.
Picture 3: Great minds **think** alike.

Picture 4: Many hands **make** light work.
Picture 5: The early bird **catches** the worm.
Picture 6: It's not work that **kills**, but worry.

The present simple is used in proverbs because proverbs are general statements / say what is generally accepted as true.

3 a When two people **don't agree**, it **is** wrong to blame only one of them.
You might say this if two children **are quarrelling**, and one of them **says** it**'s** all the other child's fault.
  b Something that you **are** especially **waiting** for **takes** a long time to happen – or never **happens** at all.
You might use this proverb if you **are waiting** for a long time for someone to arrive, or if you **are expecting** a letter or telephone call.
  c Things **are** more likely to go wrong when a lot of different people **are** in charge.
This proverb could be used if a lot of people **are working** together on a project – e.g. **planning** a trip – and the most important things **are forgotten** because each person **relies** on the others.
German equivalent: Zu viele Köche verderben den Brei.
  d When things **become** difficult, 'tough' people (= people who can stand a lot of trouble or difficulties) **are** especially successful. (The 'best' people **are** at their best in a crisis.) This was a favourite family saying of the US politician Joseph P. Kennedy, the father of President John F. Kennedy.
You could say this about a successful politician whose country **is going** through hard times, but who **is** ready to fight and overcome every problem.
  e You can't expect things to go well in life if you **don't make** an effort yourself. (It's no good relying on God only to help you; you must also rely on your own work.)
You could say this about people who **complain** that they **are** poor or unsuccessful, but who never **work** to improve their chances.
German equivalent: Hilf dir selbst, dann hilft dir Gott.
  f Not many people **stay** in love when they **are faced** with financial problems.
This proverb might be used if someone **marries** for money, but **leaves** his or her partner as soon as they **get** into financial difficulties.
  g Children often **show** the same characteristics as their parents.

This could be said if a boy whose father **is** an alcoholic later **becomes** an alcoholic himself. (The proverb is generally only used in reference to negative characteristics.)
German equivalent: Der Apfel fällt nicht weit vom Stamm.
  h An enemy who **escapes** may come back and attack again some time in the future. (It **is** sometimes wiser to give in than to risk losing everything.)
You might say this if a dog **escapes** from a fight with a larger dog, but later **starts** fighting again with a smaller dog.

Other well-known proverbs: Bad news **travels** fast; An apple a day **keeps** the doctor away; He who **laughs** last **laughs** longest; All**'s** well that **ends** well; Practice **makes** perfect.

2 New at university

are slowly making – are now starting – are just unpacking – contains – realize – gets – is staying – says – is still looking
are eating – is getting – feel – says – wants
register – meet – collect – go – are waiting – decide – is studying *(temporary state of activity over a long period of time)* – puts – rush – consists – don't like – explains – get – costs – is doing – leaves – sets
is standing – is waiting – doesn't know – does not – has – am managing *(i.e. at the moment)* – says – am spending

British students usually **start** university when they **are** 18. Some of them **are** lucky enough to live in a university hall of residence, where they **get** breakfast and an evening meal, but a lot of students **don't get** a place in a hall. Some even **live** in bed-and-breakfast hotels until they **find** a room somewhere else. There **are** a large number of university clubs and societies that students can join. Some students **get** grants from the state. Most students **don't have** much money and **have to** be careful not to spend too much on unnecessary things.

3 What's wrong with fastening your seatbelt?

1 Sarah **is beginning** to get used to her new life, now that she **lives / is living** apart from her husband. She **is doing** a lot of new thing: she **is trying** out new hobbies **and taking** part in courses. She **is** also **going** out with a doctor, **and enjoying** her independence. She **does not regret** leaving Macon at all.

1 Present Tense – Simple and Progressive

2 Sarah **dislikes** a lot of things about Macon and his family. They all **have** a very strict 'method' of doing things, and **hate** doing anything that **does not fit** in with their habits. They **play** a certain card game, for example, that nobody outside the familiy **understands.** They always **go** to the same restaurant, and when they **sit** down at the table, they always **arrange** everything exactly the same as it **is** at home. They **don't like** changes, risks, or experiments of any kind.

3 In lines 7–12 the progessive form is used to express what **is happening** to Sarah at this particular point in her life. The only examples of the simple form are *that doesn't mean* and *I want* (l. 9); both these verbs can only be used in the simple form because they express a state *(mean)* and an attitude/feeling *(want)*.
In lines 31–42 the simple form is used to describe the habits of Macon and his family (what they **always/often/regularly do**). *They don't believe* (l. 40) is an example of the simple form to express attitudes that do not change. The only example of the progressive form *(they're sitting,* l. 37) is used to describe the activity of the family at a particular moment (in the restaurant), as contrasted with *they sit at home* (i.e. every day).

4 (free expression of personal opinion)

5 (free expression of personal opinion)

Note on the author:

One of America's most praised contemporary novelists, **Anne Tyler** was born in Minneapolis, Minnesota, in 1941, but grew up in North Carolina. 'The Accidental Tourist' (1985), which has also been made into a successful film, is one of her best novels.

4 A British invasion?

Today **is** a beautiful autumn day/It **is** a beautiful autumn day (today). The sun **is shining,** and the owner of the 'Café des Pêcheurs' in Honfleur **is standing** out(side) on the terrace, where he **puts** up/**arranges** chairs and tables for his guests at ten o'clock every morning if the weather **is** fine/good. Two guests **are sitting** at one of the tables. They **are having** tea, and **talking** to each other – in English.
Although there **is** a lovely view of/onto/down to the old Norman harbour of Honfleur from here, the two Britons/British visitors **do not seem** (to be) particularly interested in the view/outlook. The man/husband **has (got)** a local paper in front of him, and **is looking** at/**studying** the advertisements for property; at the same time his wife **is marking** the position of houses and flats that **are** up for sale on a town plan of Honfleur. Every/Each weekend ten or twelve Britons methodically **look** for/**search** for their future holiday home in this way.
The tunnel under the English Channel/The Channel tunnel **is** already **casting** a/its shadow. At the moment property in Normandy/Property in Normandy at the moment only **costs** about half as much as in the South of England, but as/since the British **love** Normandy now more than ever/more than ever now, (the) prices **are** slowly **rising/increasing/going up.** The people of Honfleur/Honfleur's inhabitants **are not** all of the same opinion about this development. Some of them **are** pleased that their property **is getting/becoming** more valuable, but others **see** the danger that their town might turn into/become a kind of/sort of English holiday camp – which, of course, they **don't want** (at all)/– and that is something they **do not want** to happen, of course.

Advanced Exercises

1 Living as 'green' as they can?

1 a *are always talking* expresses the writer's feelings of impatience about other people.
  b *often talk* expresses a habit.
2 a *live* is used to express a state that does not change.
  b *are living* describes the way the Davies are behaving at this point in their lives.
3 a *always take* describes a habit; *are not thinking* has a dynamic meaning (wir spielen nicht mit dem Gedanken/denken momentan nicht daran).
  b *is always taking* expresses Barry's disapproval of Helen's habit; *I think* expresses his general attitude.
4 a *is being* is used with a dynamic meaning here (i.e. how Barry is behaving at this moment); *is always using* shows Helen's annoyance about Barry's habit; *do ... sometimes* is a neutral statement about herself.
  b *don't use* expresses a habit/fact; *is* and *has* express a state; *are doing* describes the way in which the Davies are behaving at the moment/at this point in their lives.
5 a *are trying* describes the efforts they are making at this particular time.

b *try* describes their regular habits (when they buy food).
6 a *have* describes a state; *are using* expresses what is happening at this point in the life of the family; *is producing* has the same function; *is* describes the state of convenience.
b *are always having* shows Helen's negative feelings about their arguments (she wishes they didn't happen); *thinks* expresses Barry's attitude; *uses* describes people's habits nowadays; *produce* expresses a fact; *am being* expresses Helen's behaviour at the moment.

2 Past Tense – Simple and Progressive

Check-up – note on the author:

Vernon Coleman is a doctor and a full-time writer on health and medical problems. He is well-known for his unusual but common-sense views. 'Mind Over Body' was published in 1989.

Basic Exercises

1 The Heffalump

1 **were talking**: 'accompanying circumstances' or 'background' to the following
finished: completed activity in the past
was eating: accompanying circumstances
said, saw: completed actions
was ... doing, lumping along: accompanying circumstances (what was happening at that particular moment)
asked, saw, said etc. (ll. 5–15): completed actions
talked: continuation of story
it **was** time: state in the past
stumped: simple past here, although the progressive form would also be possible (cf. GhE, 190 + Note)
edged: past state
didn't say, came, began, said etc. (ll. 19–30): series of events in the story
were able (l. 22): past state
was listening (l. 31): background to *looked round*
nodded, waited etc. (ll. 35–38): continuation of events in story
was wishing: accompanying circumstances (Normally *wish* is not used in the progressive form, but here it refers to an intense temporary wish at a particular time.)

2 They probably **thought** it **was** some very unusual animal, otherwise Christopher Robin would not have mentioned it. ('You don't see them often' also implies this.) They probably **imagined** it **was** a wild animal (certainly not belonging to their own circle of friends), which might be big and dangerous. (The word 'heffalump' might be a child's word for 'elephant'.) Because they **were not** sure exactly what it **was** like, they **found** the idea of it especially frightening and impressive.

Note on the author:

Alan Alexander Milne (1882–1956) is one of the most successful of all English writers. The third son of an enthusiastic schoolmaster who ran a small private school near London, Milne had a happy childhood. After his studies at Cambridge, he decided to become a writer, and was assistant editor of 'Punch' for eight years. After the First World War he wrote a number of successful plays, but his greatest success came with the publication of his books for children, especially 'Winnie-the-Pooh' (1926) and 'The House at Pooh Corner' (1928), which have made him famous all over the world. His characters, Christopher Robin (which was the name of his own son) and the toy animals, Winnie-the-Pooh, Piglet, Eeyore, Rabbit and others (all actual toys belonging to the 'real' Christopher Milne) have become a firmly established part of the English language and its mythology.

2 The clever cat

... When the fire **was burning** well, he **fetched** his pipe and the newspaper, **sat** down in a comfortable (arm)chair in front of the fire, and **started** reading. Before long, Mr Stevens' big dog **came** into the sitting-room, and when he **noticed** that a warm fire **was burning** in the grate, he **lay** down in front of it. Soon he **was sleeping** happily in front of the fire, while his master **was relaxing** in his chair.

Mr Stevens' cat also **liked** the warmth of the fire, but there **was** no room left in front of it for her. She **wondered** how she could get the dog out of the way – and suddenly a bright idea **came** to her mind. She **fetched** the dog's collar and lead, and **ran** up to Mr Stevens with them, hoping that this would persuade him to take the dog out for a walk.

3 A walk in the park

1 a One morning, while Mr Brown **was walking** through the park, he suddenly **heard** a strange noise. When he **looked** round, he **saw** a UFO up in the sky. It **was** just **preparing** to land.
  b A few moments later, he **looked** again. Now two strange creatures **were leaving** the UFO and **walking** through the park in the other direction.
  c Mr Brown **couldn't** believe his eyes! He **walked** on, and suddenly he **had** a brilliant idea. He **began** to walk faster.
  d When he **got** to town/into the town, he **walked** straight to an optician's shop, and **went** in to have an eye-test.
  e Shortly afterwards he **ran** out into the street – he certainly **felt** very excited now!
  f He **went** straight to the office of the local newspaper, **rushed** inside, and **reported** the latest news.

2 I used more simple forms, because this is a description of a series of actions in a story. I only used the progressive form a few times, for 'accompanying circumstances' *(while Mr Brown was walking...)* and activities going on at the same time *(two strange creatures were leaving...)*.

4 At the station

I **arrived** at the station a few minutes late, and while I **was putting** the/my money/coin/penny in the machine for the/my platform ticket, I **tried** to remember the girl. I **stood** near/by/next to the steps (leading) to the platform, and **thought**: blond(e)/fair-haired, (aged) twenty/twenty years old, (she's) coming to the town to be a teacher/to teach; and when I **looked** closely at the people who **were walking/walked** past me, it **seemed** to me as if/as though the world **were/was** full of blonde, twenty-year-old girls – so many (of them) **were coming** from/off this train, and they all **had** cases in their hands/**were** all **carrying** cases, and **looked** as if they **were coming** to the town to be teachers. I **lit** a cigarette and **went** to the other side of the steps, and I **saw/noticed** that behind the railing a girl **was sitting** on a case/and I **saw** a girl sitting on a case behind the railing.

5 Alice in the Duchess's kitchen

1 (the kitchen) **was** full of smoke
the Duchess **was sitting** on a three-legged stool
(she was) **nursing** a baby
the cook **was leaning** over the fire
(the cook was) **stirring** a large cauldron
the baby **was sneezing and howling**
a large cat ... **was sitting** on the hearth
(it was) **grinning** from ear to ear.

The progressive form is used for most of this description, because it describes the 'background' to Alice's action (i.e. when she **came in**). It also describes several activities going on at the same time. (The present participles in this scene – *nursing* and *stirring* – can be seen as contracted forms of the past progressive.)

2 The cook **took** the cauldron/pot off the fire and **began** to throw things at the Duchess and the baby; the fire-irons **came** first; saucepans, plates and dishes **followed**. The Duchess **took** no notice when they **hit** her.
Here the simple past is used to describe a series of actions in the story.

3 'The scene that I **saw** in the kitchen when I **came** in, **was** very strange. The Duchess **was sitting** on a stool with a baby, and the cook **was stirring** a big pot of soup. The air **smelt** of pepper, which **made** me sneeze – and the baby **was** either **sneezing or crying** all the time. There **was** a large cat in the kitchen, too. It **was grinning** from ear to ear. I **asked** the Duchess why it **did** this, and she **told** me that **was** because it **was** a Cheshire cat! She **got** quite rude when I **told** her I **didn't think** *any* cats **could** grin. So I **thought** it would be best to change the subject. But at that moment the cook suddenly **started** throwing things at the Duchess and the baby – fire-irons, saucepans, plates and dishes! What chaos! Some of the things **hit** them, but the Duchess **didn't seem** to mind, and the baby **went** on crying just the same as before.'

Note on the author:

Charles L. Dodgson (1832–98), who wrote under the pen-name of **'Lewis Carroll',** was one of eleven children; his family were very interested in literature and art, and they even produced their own family magazines containing stories, word games and puzzles. Dodgson went to Oxford University, where he later taught mathematics. His most famous work, 'Alice's Adventures in Wonderland', was published in 1865; the original idea for the story had come to him while he was out on a boat trip with a friend's young daughters, Lorina, Alice and Edith. In 1871, 'Through the Looking-Glass and What Alice Found There' followed. Both books were a great success, probably because – unlike most children's stories written at that time – they had no 'moral' and did not try to 'teach' anything.

Advanced Exercises

1 Different form – different meaning

'Ben **stood** up ...' means that as soon as I came into the room, he stood up. (German: Ben stand auf, ...) 'Ben **was standing** up ...' means that he was not sitting on his chair at the moment when I came in. In the first example, one action follows another. In the second example, 'background' information is given to the action of coming in. (German: Ben stand, ...)

1 **ran:** As soon as they saw us, they **ran away.** ('were running' is unlikely, but would also be possible: they were already 'in motion' at the time when they saw us.)
2 **was rising:** describes the background to the action of setting off. (As the sun rises so slowly, 'rose' – meaning a sudden action – could hardly be used here.)
3 **woke:** I **was woken up** by the sound of the alarm. ('was waking' could only be used if the speaker means the gradual development of waking up – as a background to the sudden 'action' of the alarm.)
4 **did not speak:** as this refers to a fact (she **couldn't speak** English), only the simple form can be used. ('was not speaking' – at that moment – would make no sense in the context.)
5 **made:** As soon as they came in, she **made** the coffee; one action is followed by another. ('was making' is also possible; it would mean that she was in the process of making coffee at exactly the time when they arrived – this implies that the visitors were expected, and she was preparing for their arrival.)
6 **were going:** They **were just leaving** at the moment of the telephone call. ('went', although possible in theory, is unlikely, as it implies that they **heard** the telephone, but then decided to leave the house instead of answering it!)
7 **hid:** describes the dog's action every time a thunderstorm started. ('was hiding' is hardly possible here.)
8 **sat:** He **sat down** on the eggs (by accident!) – a sudden action, probably followed by quickly moving away from the broken eggs! ('was sitting' is possible, but suggests a ridiculous situation. In German different verbs are used for the two forms: *sat = setzte sich – was sitting = saß*.)
9 **were doing:** An alibi is implied here (What **were you doing** at the time of the crime?). ('did' is less likely; it would mean what **action** you took **after** the crime took place. – e.g. **Did you call** the police?)
10 **got:** The climb is over, and 'got' describes what **happened** to us on the way up (the **state** we got into). ('were getting' would only make sense – as a 'background' – if the sentence were continued: 'we were getting very tired **when we reached the top.**')

2 Richard Cory

1 a He **made** people / us feel excited. / He made our hearts beat faster.
   b He **looked** perfect when he **was** out in the street. / There **was** something brilliant about his appearance and his way of walking.
   c His manners **were** perfect; he **knew** exactly how to behave.

2 a Richard Cory's appearance **was** very pleasing; he **behaved** like a gentleman. Although he **looked** and **seemed** so perfect in every way, and although he **was** wealthy, he **did not act** as if he were superior.
   b They **admired** his appearance and his manners, and **envied** him because they **felt** he **was** everything they would like to be themselves.
   c They **were** only **able to** see his outward appearance; they **could** not know anything about his inner life (what he **thought** and **felt**).
   d Perhaps he **committed** suicide because he **felt** lonely / unhappy / **had** no real friends / **had** some problems that nobody **knew** about / that he **was not able to** share with anyone.

3 The poet uses only the simple form because he wants to describe past happenings ('Whenever Richard Cory **went** down town, we ... **looked** at him' / 'we **worked** and **waited**') and states ('He **was** a gentleman' / 'he **was** rich'). There is no reason to describe any 'background' or 'accompanying circumstances' to particular past events.

3 Present Perfect – Simple and Progressive

Note on the author:

Edward Arlington Robinson (1869–1935) was born in Maine, and wrote many volumes of poetry, particularly about life in New England. At the age of 17, he records that he became 'violently excited over the structure and music of English blank verse', and was especially influenced by Thomas Hardy and Robert Browning. His poetry is known for its dry, sometimes ironic tone, and for its skilful use of traditional forms. He won the Pulitzer Prize for poetry three times, and during the 1920s he was generally considered to be the best living poet in America.

3 Present Perfect – Simple and Progressive

Basic Exercises

1 Junior doctors' long hours

1 ... over the past two years they **have been doing** ...: progressive form for activities that began in the past – two years ago – and are still continuing

Plans ... **have** so far **been** slow: simple form with 'so far' to describe states that began in the past and have continued into the present

Studies **have shown** ...: simple form to stress a result – i.e. it is **now** known ...

(the time) ... which **has increased** by several hours a week: simple form to show a result – i.e. they are working several hours longer **now**

The doctors **have asked** ...: simple form to express the result of a past activity on the present – i.e. the doctors are still waiting for their problem to be solved

The BMA **has suggested** ...: resultative use – i.e. their suggestion may lead to a change in the length of the working week

... this **has been accepted** ...: resultative use – i.e. the government agrees to the suggestion

I**'ve been working** for seven days ...: progressive form for activities begun in the past, which have continued – at intervals – up to the time of speaking

Since last Friday I**'ve been** on call for 122 hours ...: simple form to describe a state that began in the past, and has continued up to the time of speaking

... you feel as is you**'ve** just **crossed** the Atlantic: simple form for activities only just completed

... the pilot **has been working** since Friday: progressive form for activities begun in the past and still continuing

2 Recently junior doctors' hours **have increased**. Over the past two years they **have been working** up to five hours a week longer. Studies **have shown/proved** a connection between overwork and mistakes calculating drug doses.

The doctors **have asked** for clerks to take over routine work, and the BMA **has suggested** a maximum working week of 72 hours.

The government **has agreed** in principle (but health authorities would need more staff).

Keith Altman, a junior doctor, feels exhausted when he **has been working** for days and nights on end. He feels as if he **has** just **crossed** the Atlantic.

3 Keith Altman, diensthabender Assistenzarzt in einem Krankenhaus in Stevenage, sagte letzten Donnerstag um 19 Uhr: ‚Ich arbeite schon seit sieben Tagen und vier Nächten und ich bin total kaputt/fühle mich völlig erschöpft. Seit letzten Freitag habe ich 122 – von insgesamt 152 Stunden – Bereitschaftsdienst gehabt. Nach einem Wochenende im Dienst fühlt man sich so, als hätte man gerade den Atlantik überquert – es ist als ob man unter Jetlag litte/es ist so wie wenn man nach einem langen Flug Schwierigkeiten mit der Zeitumstellung hat. Es ist kein vernünftiges System – weder für uns noch für die Patienten. Stellen Sie sich vor, montag morgens in einem Flugzeug mit einer Maschine zu fliegen, obwohl Sie wissen/und zu wissen, daß der Pilot seit Freitag arbeitet/im Einsatz ist – Sie würden es nicht tun, stimmt's? Nun, so ist ungefähr die Situation.'

4 '... I**'ve been working** on the ward for 14 hours, and I**'ve** just **got** myself a cup of coffee/tea. I**'ve** only just **left** the ward, and I**'ve started** talking to one of the nurses.'

'The next picture is of me at quarter to three in the morning. I**'ve** just **been called** to a cardiac arrest./

I've just **picked** up the telephone, only to hear that one of the patients **has suffered** a cardiac arrest. So my 'break' **has finished** already. **I haven't had** much of a rest.'

2 The new evangelism

'**I've been going** to church regularly since my childhood/since I was a child,' says Patty Schwarz from Nashville, Tennessee. 'Sunday **has** always **been** the highlight/high point/big day of the week for me. I've also **made** a lot of friends through (the) church/through going to church.'
Patty and her family, like approximately 25 million other Americans, are 'evangelists'. In their belief, it is not enough just/simply to accept the teachings of Christianity; you have to be 'born again'. You aren't/can't be 'born again' until you **have recognized** Christ personally as your Lord – and (your) life **has taken** on a new meaning./Not until you **have recognized** ..., are you born again – and your life ...
For some years (now), leading evangelists **have been using** television to spread their interpretation of the word of God among the population. This **has proved** very effective. But the so-called 'tele-evangelists' and their highly emotional programmes **have** often **been criticised** recently./But recently ... some well-known 'tele-evangelists' **have** even **appeared** in an unfavourable light because of fraud and dishonesty.
'But all this/that has nothing to do with my belief,' says Patty. 'Nothing **has changed** for me personally, or for my friends.'/'For me personally, and for my friends, nothing **has changed**.'

Note:
The photo shows 'tele-evangelist' Jimmy Swaggart.

3 The tooth

1 a) a saying that everyone **has heard** of/a proverb that people **have been using** for years; b) what someone **has experienced**/what **has happened** to a person at the dentist's; c) a secret plan to keep quiet that **has been agreed** on /**made** by (all) dentists/that dentists **have agreed** on.

2 'This sort of thing **has been going on** ever since ...' refers to events that started to happen many years ago, and still keep on happening.
'However many years it may be that dentists **have been plying** their trade' refers to the dentists' work that began years ago and is still being done.

'... the narrator who **has suffered** so' refers to past events and their effect on the patient (resultative use).
'People **have never tired** of talking about their teeth' is a general statement referring to what has never (so far) taken place.

3 For years and years people/journalists/authors/writers **have been writing** little articles on the subject, and people **have been making** little jokes./... people **have been writing** little articles **and making** little jokes on the subject.

4 a '... One of my fillings **has come** out/**has broken** off.'
b '... I've been going there twice a year ever since I can remember, and **I haven't had** any trouble so far/nothing terrible **has happened** so far.'
c 'One of my wisdom teeth **has been pulled**/**taken** out.'
d '... **I haven't been** (there) for ages.'
e '... now that those modern drills **have been invented**/**have replaced** the old-fashioned ones.'
f '... I've been using ... (name of product) for years ...'

Advanced Exercises

1 The present perfect without adverbials of time

1 '... He**'s been drinking**.'
2 '... I**'ve broken** one of those new plates.'
3 '**Have** you **found** the book ...?'
4 'I**'ve been taking** the dog for a walk.'
5 '... **Have** you **been crying?**'
6 'Yes, I**'ve learnt** them all.'
7 'My father **has been learning** German ...'
8 '... I**'ve spent** all my pocket money.'

2 Summing up the situation

1 (phrase-book) There **has been** an accident. The British car/The British driver **has knocked** a Frenchman off his bike. It looks as if the car **has been driving** on the wrong side of the road. The bike **has been damaged**, but it doesn't look as if the cyclist **has been injured**.
2 (snowman) The children's father **has been making**/**building** a snowman. He **has finished** it now. He **has been working** on it for hours, and he **has**

4 Past Tense and Present Perfect Contrasted

made it look really good. So naturally he is annoyed because the children **haven't helped** him. They **haven't** even **been** outside – or looked at what he **has done**. They **have been watching** TV all the time instead.

3 (ski-hotel) The man / skier **has broken** his leg / **has had** a skiing accident. His leg **has been put** in plaster. The people in the rooms on the second floor **have** each **put** one shoe out to be cleaned. So it looks as if they **have** all **had** skiing accidents, too.

4 Past Tense and Present Perfect Contrasted

Basic Exercises

1 Acid mist pollution

Past tense	Present perfect
	have blamed – result is still important
	have *repeatedly* **blamed** – expression of frequency used; the result, not the exact time is important
damaged – signal: *last month*	
were responsible for the acid mist which **affected** ... – signal: *on September 9th*	
	There **has not been** ... – signal: *since Chernobyl*
rolled ... **affected** – refer to a specific event in the past	
killed – signal: *overnight*	
	There **have** also **been** *repeated* cases – this has often happened; the exact time is not referred to
was working ... when the mist **arrived** – action in progress at a certain time in the past when a new event took place *(arrived)*	
said – refers to a certain point in time	
started – signal: *a week later*	
were turning brown – gradual development / event in progress at a certain time in the past	
	have been investigating – action started in the past, still in progress
	have discovered – result is important in the present
	have been wondering – this began in the past and still continues to be so
	have blamed – exact time not important; the possible effect on people's health is stressed
	have not been able – 'so far' is implied

2 a Acid mist from the Continent **affected** 1,000 square miles of the east coast of Britain and **damaged** thousand of trees. Fumes from cars and heavy industry in East Germany, Poland and West Germany **caused** this case of air pollution.

b It **killed** the leaves on trees and hedges, and possibly **caused** colds and cases of irritation of the skin and eyes.
c The worst case of air pollution (at the time the text was written) **was** in the spring of 1986, when there **was** an accident at the nuclear power station in Chernobyl in the USSR (cf. l. 10).
Fumes from heavy industry, etc. **have been blamed** for acid rain which **has caused** damage to forests, especially reported in Germany. Britain **has been** partly responsible for this. Fumes from cars and other vehicles **have** also **caused** a lot of pollution in Europe (cf. ll. 4–6).
Worldwide (up to 1991) the most terrible case of air pollution **has been caused** by the burning of Kuwaiti oilfields deliberately set fire to by Saddam Hussein during the war in the Persian Gulf.
d Not enough **has been done** yet, but certain improvements **have been made.** Unleaded petrol **has been introduced,** and catalytic converters **have been installed** in cars. Sprays etc. that attack the ozone layer **have been banned,** and cleaner methods of production **have begun** to replace the old ones. People **have** generally **become** more conscious of the need for environment-friendly products and methods.

2 The great moment

1 The scientists **have been working** in their laboratory since nine o'clock in the morning.
2 They **have been doing** experiments all day.
3 They **have known** each other for years.
4 Now at last they **have made** a revolutionary discovery.
5 When they **started** work in the morning, the sun **was shining** and the weather **seemed** good.
6 None of them **noticed** when the storm **started,** because they **were** all **working** so hard.
7 Now the strong wind **has uprooted** the tree outside their laboratory.
8 But they still **haven't noticed** anything yet.

3 Indian girls in Britain

has changed – arranged – have begun – weren't allowed – hated – was – have asserted – have been forced – was talking/talked – were having/had – told – was
have been working – left – have finished – didn't like – have got
overheard – was talking – said

4 Past Tense and Present Perfect Contrasted

4 Adrian, the runaway

1 In the first three cases, the *results* of what has happened are stressed: Nobody **has said** 'Happy birthday' to Adrian, so *he feels unhappy.* He **has asked** three policemen the time / **has tried** repeatedly to attract attention, but there **has been** *no result,* and Adrian's situation **has not changed.** What Adrian writes at 7.30 a.m. on Sunday is a detailed description of **a series of finished actions** in the past (**got up** at six, **had** a wash, **read** ..., etc.).

2 Seit 2 Tagen habe ich das (gesetzlich verbriefte) Recht, Zigaretten zu kaufen, Geschlechtsverkehr zu haben, Moped zu fahren und nicht zu Hause zu wohnen / wohnen zu müssen.
Mrs. Merryfield, die Frau des Pfarrers, hat meine Eltern angerufen und sie gebeten, mich hier abzuholen.
In German, the 'Präsens' is used in the first sentence (to describe a state that began in the past and has continued into the present) and the 'Perfekt' is used in the second sentence (to stress a result), whereas in English the present perfect is used in both cases.

3 a He was sitting (and having something to eat, perhaps) in the café at Manchester Railway Station, together with his dog.
b He was sitting / resting / having a rest on a park bench.
c He was trying to sleep in the church porch / lying in the church porch / writing his diary in the church porch.

4 When Adrian **arrived** in Manchester, he **went** into the station café with his dog, and **bought** himself something to eat. Later, a waitress **ordered** them to leave the café. In the afternoon Adrian **bought** himself a birthday card and **pretended** it was from his parents. He **listened** to the news on his radio at 6 p.m., and then **tried** to attract the attention of the police in various ways. He even **rang** up the police station and **gave** a description of himself, but the police **did not react** at all. Finally he **tried** to go into an Indian Restaurant for a meal, but he **was sent** away, so he **made** his way to a church, and **tried** to sleep a little in the porch.

5 'I **got** quite a surprise when I **went** down to the church this morning. Just as I **was walking** through the gravestones, I **saw** a boy of about 15 or 16 standing in the church porch – with his dog!

4 Past Tense and Present Perfect Contrasted

He **seemed** very glad to see me, and of course I **asked him what he was doing** there. Apparently he**'s run** away from home, and he**'s been** here in Manchester since Saturday morning. He **looked** quite exhausted, poor boy, so I **told** him to come along with me and have a rest here. I**'ve given** him a good breakfast and I**'ve rung** up his parents **and asked** them to come and collect him – and his dog!'

Note on the author:

Although **Sue Townsend** (born in 1946) has written a number of plays, she is best-known for her humorous fiction. Her first best-seller, 'The Secret Diary of Adrian Mole Aged 13¾', was published in 1982 and was followed in 1984 by 'The Growing Pains of Adrian Mole'. Both books were immediately praised by readers of all ages, and can be seen as classics in the literature of family life.

5 Northern Ireland – land of troubles

'A 36-year-old policeman **died** yesterday near Belfast when a bomb **exploded** under the driving seat of his car. His 8-year-old daughter, who(m) he **was** just **driving/taking** to school, **was** badly/seriously **injured**.' Such reports of violence **have been** part of everyday life in Northern Ireland for a long time now. In the last two decades there **have been** terrible attacks in (Great) Britain too. In 1974, for example, 21 people **were killed/lost** their lives in a bomb attack in Birmingham. In December 1983 the IRA **set** off a car bomb in front of Harrod's, the London department store; the explosion, which **happened/took** place at a time when a lot of people **were doing** their Christmas shopping, **killed** 5 people and **injured** 91.
Ireland's problems **started/had** their beginnings in the 16th and 17th centuries. At that time/It was then that Protestants from England and Scotland **settled** especially in the northern part of the country and **began** to suppress the Irish Catholics. The Republic of Ireland – (which is) 95% Catholic – **has been** independent of the United Kingdom since 1921, but Northern Ireland – with a Protestant majority of 65% of the population – **has remained** 'British'. In 1969 violence **broke** out on both sides in Londonderry and Belfast. Since then/Since that time, British soldiers **have been trying** to keep order in Ulster, but a solution to the problem **has not been found** yet/so far. The mistrust between Protestants and Catholics **has remained** more or less unchanged.

Advanced Exercises

1 Past tense or present perfect with certain adverbials of time and frequency

1. I **waited** for 20 minutes, ...
2. He**'s just gone** out ...
3. He**'s always hated** opera, ...
4. **Have** you **seen** Greg today?
5. It **was just coming** in ... She**'s always been** lucky ...
6. Where **did** you go ...? ... We**'ve always loved** Greece. ... I**'ve never known** it as hot as it **was** this time. ... we **never went** to the Continent. We **always had** ... and it **was never** too hot ...
7. I**'ve already seen** it ...
8. ... she **was just writing** some letters ... She**'s been sitting** up there for hours now.

2 Past tense or present perfect in sentences without time adverbials

1. I don't know where she is.
2. ... when I was in London last month.
3. ... when I was in town this morning.
4. I still remember what you told me (yesterday).
5. We haven't had a letter from him yet.
6. All this happened last week/yesterday. The trip is over now.
7. ... when I rang you up last night?/... when it rang five minutes ago?
8. I'm annoyed/worried. What am I going to do?
9. Don't you want to play tennis on holiday? (You can still pack them if you want to change your mind.)
10. You can have them while I'm out.
11. That was a long time ago./... when you were small.
12. ... when you made it?/Did you forget them (at the time when you were preparing the salad)?

5 Forms of Future

Basic Exercises

1 An unexpected invitation

1 I *expect* you**'ll be** surprised: *will*-future for what the speaker supposes
what **I'm going to suggest**; *going to* for an intention
Probably ... **won't suit you**; you *probably* **won't be able to** ...: *will*-future for what the speaker supposes
There **will be** plenty of duck here soon, *if* it **gets** cold enough: *will*-future (for a prediction) in the main clause, simple present in the *if*-clause
... **are having to** leave *shortly*: present progressive for a definite arrangement, with an adverbial of time
I**'ll** badly **need** someone else: *will*-future for a prediction
I**'m not putting** the boat ... *for a bit*: present progressive for a definite arrangement, with an adverbial of time
If you **can** come, a telegram ... **will find** me: simple present in the *if*-clause, *will*-future in the main clause
Flushing ... **will be** your best route: *will*-future for what the speaker supposes
your boat ... **goes** from Queenboro': simple present for timetable information
I'm going to have a few repairs done here *this week*: *going to* for a plan or intention, referring to the near future
... **will have** them ready by the time your train **arrives**: *will*-future (for a prediction) in the main clause, simple present in the time clause
that **will be** a great help: *will*-future for what the speaker supposes / for a prediction
I've a feeling that you**'ll come**: *will*-future for what the speaker supposes
I**'ll be** here when you **get** here: *will*-future (for a promise) in the main clause, simple present in the *when*-clause

2 a He**'s going to** do some yachting and duckshooting. But first he**'s going to have** a few repairs done to his boat.
 b He wants Carruthers to join him because his friends in Germany **are leaving** shortly, and he**'ll need** someone else to help him with the boat.
 c He doesn't know what Carruthers **is going to do** / is planning to do in the next few weeks; he thinks Carruthers probably **won't be** able to leave the Foreign Office / **won't get** time off for the trip to Germany.
 d He **will need** waterproof clothes for the yachting and duckshooting.

3 a 'Which London station **does** the train to Queenboro' **go** from?'
 'When **does** it **leave** London?'
 '**Do** I **have to** change trains?'
 '**Is** there / **Will** there **be** a sleeping car / a restaurant car on the train?'
 '**Will** I **have to** make a reservation?'
 '**Will** there **be** any trouble getting a seat?'
 'How long **does** the crossing **take**?'
 'When **does** the boat **get** to Flushing?' (etc.)
 b The weather **will** probably **be** cool, so I**'ll need** some warm clothes.
 I**'ll** probably **need** a map of the area.
 I**'ll take** my camera.
 I**'ll** certainly **need** my sailing shoes.
 I**'ll pack** some writing paper, in case I want to write some letters while I**'m** away.
 I**'ll** probably **have** time for a bit of reading, so I**'ll take** a book or two.
 I suppose I**'ll need** clothes for the evening. / If Davies and I **go** out in the evening, I**'ll need** the right clothes for that. (etc.)

Note on the author:

Erskine Childers (1870–1922), a writer and a political activist, was a Clerk in the House of Commons for 15 years. Later he settled in Ireland, and in 1921 he became 'director of publicity' for the Irish Republicans. In 1922 he was court-martialled and shot by firing squad. He is especially remembered for his novel 'The Riddle of the Sands', published in 1903.

2 Are you coming this evening?

Sandra: **Are** you **coming / going to come** to the clubhouse this evening / tonight? There**'ll** probably **be** a new ladies' team next year, and we**'re** all **meeting / going to meet** to talk about / discuss the details (together).
Julia: I'm afraid I **won't manage** it this time. I**'m going** to choir tonight. We**'re rehearsing** with the orchestra for the concert on Saturday. There**'ll be** trouble if I **don't go**.

5 Forms of Future

Sandra: When **does** your rehearsal **start** (then)?
Julia: At half past seven. It **will** probably **go** on until nine or half past (nine). By then the meeting at the clubhouse **will** definitely / most probably / certainly **be** over. / The meeting is sure / certain to be over by then.
Sandra: I don't think it **will!** / I don't think so. We**'re not meeting** / **not going to meet** until half past eight. So if you **come** to the clubhouse after the rehearsal, the meeting **will** probably **be** still in full swing.
Julia: All right. I**'ll come** as soon as the rehearsal **is** over.

3 He's leaving home

1 He**'s leaving** after breakfast. He**'s going** on the road. He**'s hitchhiking,** and he**'s not taking** any luggage. He**'s** only **taking** ten dollars with him, but he's planning to be away for five or ten years. He has no idea where he**'s going,** but he plans / wants to spend the rest of his life with simple people.

2 If he **stays** at college, he**'ll** just **spend** all day working in classrooms and libraries / he **won't get** to know the kind of people he feels interested in / ...
If he **becomes** a teacher, he**'ll** never **get** to know about 'real' life outside the classroom / he**'ll spend** all his life in classrooms and schools / ...
He's afraid that he**'ll waste** his life if he **stays** at college / ...
He feels that living and working with simple people **will** probably **be** more interesting and rewarding / ...
By breaking away, he expects that he **will be** able to make his life more worthwhile / that he **will get** to know 'better' people / ...

3 (free expression of opinion)

4 The author uses the present progressive most, to express Benjamin's immediate arrangements and plans. In some places, the *going-to*-future could have been used instead, e.g. 'I**'m not going to take** any luggage', to express a plan or intention.

Note on the author:

Born in San Francisco in 1939, **Charles Webb** graduated in American history and literature at Williams College, Massachusetts. 'The Graduate', published in 1963, was his first novel, and a great success; it tells the story of a young man's search for identity, and has been described as 'a brilliantly sordid tale'. It was filmed in 1967 with Dustin Hoffman in the title-role. Webb has written several other novels, and has had a number of different jobs.

Advanced Exercises

1 The future of the world

1 **Text A:** The sun **is** never **going to hurt** us ... (l. 1)
Text C: ... there **are going to be** 10 billion people on the Earth. It**'s going to be** hard to feed those people ... (ll. 15–16)
The *going-to*-future is suitable here because it expresses a logical conclusion. (In Text A this is based on scientific observation of the sun's 'behaviour' so far, and on experience gained from the 'behaviour' of other stars; in Text C the 'inevitable' results of world population growth are expressed).

2 10 billion people **will be living** on the Earth, probably in a completely different climate. The people on Earth **will be finding** it impossible to provide food for everyone, and they **will be trying** to prevent each other from using nuclear weapons.

3 The sun **will have set.**
The sun **will have risen.**
The sun **will have become** much bigger and redder / **will have become** so bright and big that it **will have ended** / **put** an end to all life on Earth.
Life on Earth **will have come** to an end / **will have stopped** / **will have died** out altogether.

4 The Earth's population **will have reached** 10 billion. The climate w**ill have changed,** and a period of drought **will have started** / **set** in. People **will be starving.** People from third-world countries **will be invading** Europe. Tuvalu **will have disappeared** under the sea / **will have sunk** into the sea, and its people **will have moved** to Australia or New Zealand. A lot of other islands **will** also **have disappeared.**
(etc. – free expression of own ideas here)

2 It's inevitable

1 There **is going to be** an accident. The two cars **are going to crash** / **collide.**
2 There **are going to be** lots of apples on the trees in the autumn. / It**'s going to be** a good year for apples.
3 It**'s going to be** an exciting / interesting match.

4 It**'s going to be**/**We're going to have** a rough crossing. A lot of people **are going to be** seasick.
5 There **is going to be** a shortage of water./Water **is going to be** a problem/in short supply. People **are going to have to** save water.
6 The train **is going to be** very full. It**'s going to be** difficult to get a seat.

3 Gone! A Victorian melodrama

1 In one minute Henry **will be sitting** in a comfortable armchair, and the cook **will be making** him some tea. In five minutes he **will be having** a cup of tea, and the cook **will be talking** to him/**will be trying** to cheer him up. He **will be telling** her all about Louisa.

2 An hour later Louisa **will have got** back home. She **will be wishing** she hadn't thrown the jewels out of the window/**will be wondering** what has happened to Henry/**will be feeling** glad that she has got rid of Henry at last/...
Henry **will have finished** his tea/**will have left** the house again. He **will be feeling** better/**will be thinking** about Louisa and the jewels/**will be wondering** what he ever saw in Louisa/...
Six months later Louisa **will have married** someone else/...
Henry **will have forgotten** about Louisa/**will have met** someone else/...
Louisa and Henry **will have got** married after all. They **will be living** together happily/...
(etc.)

6 Sequence of Tenses

Basic Rules – note on the authors:

James Laver was born in 1899, and educated at Oxford University. An expert on the history of costume, he has also written plays, poetry and short stories.

Daphne du Maurier (1907–1989) was born in London and educated in Paris. Many of her popular novels, including the world-famous 'Rebecca' (1938), are set in the South-West of England, where she spent many years of her life.

Basic Exercises

1 Sleep: How much do you need?

goes off – has been proved – need – are getting/get – need – have had
allow – will compensate – have lost (or: their bodies **compensate** for the sleep they **lose** – this version expresses a general statement of fact, rather than the natural consequence expressed in the version with *will*).
had – fall – are driving – do not remember – happened
have had – hate – are – will sleep – suffer – go will feel – do

2 A bright idea

One lovely summer afternoon, Mr Bright **went** out into the garden. The weather during the last few months **had been** very hot and dry, so he **decided** to water the flowers in the big flowerbed. After he **had got** the hosepipe out of the garage, he **switched** on the water. But when he **started** to spray the plants, he **noticed** that a hole **had developed** in the hosepipe. At first he **felt** rather annoyed because he **realized** that the hosepipe **would have to** be repaired. Then he suddenly **had** a bright idea. He **went** back to the house and **fetched** a corkscrew which he **had used** the evening before to open a bottle of wine. As soon as he **had switched** the water off, he **started** work: he **made** a neat row of little holes in the hosepipe. He really **enjoyed** the job because all the time he **was thinking** of the work that he **would save** himself. After he **had finished** the job, he **switched** the water back on, then **stood** back to admire the results. The water jets **worked** beautifully! Mr Bright **had** nothing else to do, so he **thought** he **would relax** for the rest of the afternoon. He **fetched** a deckchair, and shortly after he **had sat** down, his eyes **closed** and he **fell** asleep.

3 The newcomer

1 Day **had broken**... (l. 1); the way he **had come** (ll. 6–7); the ice jams... **had formed** (ll. 10–11);

6 Sequence of Tenses

this spittle **had crackled** in the air (l. 24); They **had come** over ... (l. 29); he **had come** the roundabout way (ll. 30–31); A foot of snow **had fallen** since the last sled **had passed** over (ll. 42–43); The frozen moisture ... **had settled** on its fur (ll. 47–48).

In each case, the past perfect is used to describe events that took place at an earlier time, in contrast to the past tense, which is used for the chronological account of events in the story.

2 Conditional forms are used to refer to a later time / to refer to the 'future' – from the man's point of view / to describe what the man expects to happen later in the day.

3 Although the weather **was** extremely cold, the man **had** never **been** in the Yukon before, so he **did not realize** how low the temperature actually **was**. He **was not** able to imagine what **would happen** if he **walked** a long way in such conditions. He simply **did not know** how foolish it **was** to be outside for nine hours when it **was** so tremendously cold.

4 The dog **had lived / had been living** in a cold climate for years, and it **knew** the dangers because it **had experienced** such low temperatures before. It also **knew** by instinct how dangerous the situation **was / could be**.

5 ... and he **wants** to join his friends in camp that evening. They **have gone** a different way, so he **is** alone. It **is** very cold, but the man, a newcomer in the Yukon, **does not realize** how dangerous it **is** to travel long distances at such low temperatures. Even when his spittle **crackles** in the air before it **falls** to the snow, he **believes** the temperature **is** of no importance. He just **thinks** happily of the food he **is carrying** with him, and **looks** forward to reaching camp where the others **will be waiting** for him. The man **has** no sled with him, but a big husky. The dog **does not like** the cold, which it **realizes is** extremely dangerous, and which the man **has** completely **underestimated**. In reality, the temperature **is** 75 below zero.

Note on the author:

Jack Griffith (1876–1916), born in San Francisco, took the name of his stepfather, John **London**. He grew up in poverty and without proper schooling; as a teenager he earned his living – legally and illegally – as a factory worker, an 'oyster pirate' and a sailor, and later he took part in the Klondike gold rush of 1897. He had a passionate interest in reading, and his own varied experiences gave him the material for his stories. 'The Call of the Wild' (1903) and 'The Sea-Wolf' (1904), both novels, made him hugely popular, and during the last 16 years of his life he wrote about fifty books. Of these, the collections of short stories are probably most likely to be remembered.

Advanced Exercises

1 The party dress

1. a Some of the girls **had been looking** forward to this ..., but Clara **had been dreading** it. (ll. 1–3)
   b (She) **had had** nothing resembling a party dress since the age of six, when she **had possessed** a fetching little garment ... (ll. 5–6)
   c (Her mother) **had tried** to instil into her children the view that the truly refined can manage ... (ll. 14–15)
   d Her mother **had reacted** to the subject in a predictable way, and **had expatiated** at some length ..., but in the end she **had consented** ... (ll. 17–21)

2. a 'What she **did**' = 'What she **had done**.'
   'where she **discovered**' = 'where she **had discovered**'
   'She **came** downstairs' = 'She **had come** downstairs'
   'Clara's spirits faintly **rose**' = '... **had** faintly **risen**'
   'the colour ... **was** one ...' = 'the colour ... **had been** one ...'
   'she rather **fancied**' = 'she **had** rather **fancied**'
   'her spirits **sank**' = 'her spirits **had sunk**'
   b What she *did* was to go through her cupboards, where she *discovered* a dress which **had** once **belonged** to Clara's cousin, and which **had been enclosed** before in a charitable parcel of hand-ons.
   The incident of looking through the cupboards is a flashback referring to the time directly before the trip to Paris. But the two verbs in the past perfect **(had belonged, had been enclosed)** refer to an earlier date, and create a 'flashback within a flashback'.
   c 'But once she **had tried** it on, ...' (l. 27) = 'But once she **tried** it on, ...'

3. a anxious to display clothes *that* **had been bought** by extravagant parents.

b not to try to ask her mother *whether she **could/might/would buy** her a new dress.*
c Her mother had reacted to the subject *just as Clara **had expected**/as she **would have predicted**.*
d about *how absurd it **was** to take* a dress all the way to Paris.
e not unwilling to please *with pleasure that she **had bought** so cheaply/that **had been bought** so cheaply/that **had cost** her so little.*

4 a 'I'm dreading it actually, because I haven't got anything nice to wear. I've only got an awful old dress that used to belong to my cousin.'
b 'I didn't want to ask her because I knew she would be against buying anything for me, and I could imagine exactly how she would react.'
c 'No, I'm afraid she doesn't. She tends to think that things like new clothes or extras like entertainments are a waste of money. She thinks spending money is vulgar.'

Note on the author:

Born in Sheffield in 1939, **Margaret Drabble** went to a boarding school in York, and then to Cambridge University, where she studied English. She is well-known as a novelist. 'Jerusalem the Golden', published in 1967, was one of her early works. But she has also written critical studies of Wordsworth and Arnold Bennett, and has given lectures for the Arts Council and the British Council. She edited a new edition of 'The Oxford Companion to English Literature' in 1985, which is a highly praised work of reference.

2 South coast anglers ready for Jaws

1 **Incident 1:** A lifeguard **saw** a shark swimming among bathers at Salcombe in Devon, and quickly **hustled** them out of the water. (ll. 8–9; ll. 32–34)
Incident 2: An experienced fisherman/fishing boat skipper from Plymouth **saw** a very large shark following his boat. The anglers on board **had been gutting** fish and the shark **was following** the waste they **had thrown** into the sea. (ll. 1–4; ll. 12–17; ll. 21–23)
Incident 3: Divers **saw** a large Mako shark in Plymouth Sound. (ll. 27–30)
Incident 4 (unlike the first three, only involving a dead shark): Crowds of people **looked** on while five men **struggled** with a netted porbeagle shark at Plymouth market. (ll. 38–40)

2 a He **believes** there **is** a giant shark swimming about off the Devon coast. He **fears** that someone **will/may** soon **be attacked.** (ll. 3–7)
b Some shark fishermen **agree** there **is** a danger of sharks coming close to beaches – and possibly attacking swimmers – if warmer weather **affects** sea temperatures. (ll. 9–11)
Another Plymouth skipper **agrees** that sharks **come** closer to shore than most people **realize.** (ll. 35–36)
But marine biologists and many other anglers **do not believe** there **are** such large sharks in British waters. They **think** the stories **are exaggerated.** (ll. 24–25)
Conservationists **are** against excessive angling of sharks. (ll. 43–44)
An expert on fish at the Natural History Museum **thinks** people's fear of sharks **is** unreasonable, and that shark attacks in British waters **are** extremely unlikely. (ll. 45–52)
(+ free expression of personal opinion)

3 Last year, in an incident *which **was** hardly **reported**/which **was not given** much publicity* a lifeguard hustled bathers from a British beach *after he **had seen*** a shark *that **was swimming*** among them.

4 a a skipper who **has been fishing/following** his trade for many years/who **has had** lots of experience.
b a skipper who **has been sailing** in the Plymouth area for 19 years/who **has been** a Plymouth fisherman for 19 years.
c the way (in which) they **fight**.
d fish that **have weighed** 350 pounds.
e a porbeagle shark which **had been netted/had been caught** in a net.

5 'Jaws' **is** about an enormous shark that **comes** close to the shore and **attacks** and **kills** bathers at a seaside resort on the East coast of the USA. After a series of frightening incidents, the shark **is hunted** down by three men (the local chief of police, a marine biologist, and an experienced fisherman). There **is** an exciting – and bloody – battle with the shark, in which the fisherman **is killed,** before the vicious shark **is** finally **defeated.**
(+ free expression of personal experience)

7 Conditional Sentences

Basic Exercises

1 I'm in a 'What if' mood today

1 He uses 'Type II' because the condition isn't very likely to be fulfilled (he isn't seriously thinking of marrying Arlene).

2 a 'I wonder what **will happen** if I **marry** Arlene. We**'ll have** a huge wedding. Then we**'ll raise** some kittens, and they**'ll crawl** all over me ... I**'ll make** a lousy father.'
In this case, Garfield is seriously considering marriage, and imagining a very real future. (However, the last sentence doesn't sound very logical with the future tense after 'Forget it!')

b '... what **would have happened** if I **had married** Arlene. We **would have had** a huge wedding ... **would have raised** ... they **would have crawled** ... I **would have made** a lousy father.'
Here, Garfield is thinking back on a situation in the past (before he decided **not** to marry Arlene) – and of what consequences there would have been.

3 'If we **had** some kittens, I**'d have to** spend some of my time looking after them. I**'d be** much busier than I am now. John **would have to** buy more cat food. ...'
'If I **stayed** on my own, I**'d be** much happier really / things **would be** much simpler.'
'If Arlene **wasn't** so beautiful, I**'d** never **think** of getting married anyway.'

2 Do you know this joke?

pull – he'll say; pull – he'll say ('he says ...' is also possible, as a general statement);
  will happen – pull – I'll fall (or: would happen – pulled – I'd fall; 'Type II' is also possible here, as a hypothetical question by the boy)
prefer – I'll pull
would serve – forgot (or: will serve – forget)
stand – will flow ('flows' also possible, as a general statement)
had – wouldn't hurry
don't (do so) – will come

3 Things would be much better if ...

1 a ... if your hair **was** shorter.
 b ... **we'd be** able to afford a holiday in Spain.
 c ... we**'ll** soon **have** no money left at all.
 d ... you **would achieve** much more.
 e ... I **would have been** able to offer some to Betsy.
 f ... if you **were** more cheerful / less bossy.
 g ... we **wouldn't have had** to hurry so much.
 h ... I **would have been** able to wear / **could have worn** them now.
 i ... if you **forget** to look in the mirror.

2 a If you **use** my balls again, you**'ll have to** buy me some new ones.
 b If you**'d woken** me up, I **wouldn't have been** late for school.
 c If he/she **called** on me, I**'d find** the lessons more interesting.
 d I **wouldn't have copied** your work if I**'d known** you minded.
 e I **would have scored** a goal if you**'d passed** me the ball.
 f If you **like** wearing it so much, I**'ll give** it to you for Christmas.
 g We **would have been** able to go to the concert if I**'d remembered** to book tickets.
 h Nothing **would have happened** if I**'d checked** the brakes.

4 Once upon a time

1 *Summary of the story of Little Red Riding Hood:*
Grandmother was ill, so Little Red Riding Hood's mother baked a cake for her, and gave it to Little Red Riding Hood to take to her grandmother's house. On the way to the house, Little Red Riding Hood stopped in the wood to pick some flowers, and a wolf came up to her and asked where she was going. Red Riding Hood told the Wolf she was going to see her grandmother, and explained where she lived. When he heard this, the Wolf ran quickly to Grandmother's house, went inside, attacked Grandmother and ate her up. Then he changed into her night clothes and got into her bed, where he waited for Little Red Riding Hood to come in. When she arrived, he pretended to be her grandmother, and when she came up to the bed, he pounced on her and ate her up. (The English version of the tale ends here.)

Comment:
If the Wolf **hadn't spoken** English, he **wouldn't have been able to** talk to Little Red Riding Hood.

7 Conditional Sentences

If she **hadn't talked** to him, he **would** never **have found** out where her grandmother lived.
If the Wolf **hadn't been** so hungry, he **wouldn't have eaten** Grandmother up.
If Little Red Riding Hood **hadn't been** so naive, she **would have realized** it was the Wolf in her grandmother's night clothes.
(If the Hunter **hadn't come** to the rescue, the story **would have ended** here ...)

2 *Snow White:*
If the Queen **hadn't been** so vain *(eitel)*, she **wouldn't have been** so jealous of Snow White.
If Snow White **hadn't bitten** into the apple, she **wouldn't have been** poisoned. If the dwarfs *(Zwerge)* **had been** at home, they **would have protected** Snow White from the evil Queen.
(*other useful words:* mirror, witch, coffin, funeral)

Sleeping Beauty:
If the Bad Fairy **had been invited** to the christening party *(Tauffeier)*, she **wouldn't have cast** the wicked spell *(Zauber)* on the baby Princess.
If the Princess **hadn't pricked** her finger on a spindle (at the spinning wheel), she **would not have fallen** asleep for a hundred years.
If the Prince **hadn't cut** through the hedge, he **wouldn't have managed** to get to the castle and rescue the Princess from her sleep.
(*other useful words:* banquet, thorns)

Hansel and Gretel:
If their parents **hadn't been** so poor, they **would** never **have tried** to get rid of the children.
If the little birds **hadn't eaten** all the breadcrumbs, the children **would have found** their way back home.
If Gretel **hadn't pushed** the old witch into the oven, the witch **would have baked and eaten** both the children.
(*other useful words:* gingerbread house, treasure chest)

Rumpelstiltskin:
If the miller **hadn't told** the king that his daughter could spin straw into gold, she **would** never **have been taken** to the palace.
If Rumpelstiltskin **hadn't helped** her, the straw **would** never **have been spun** into gold / the miller's daughter **would have been punished / killed.**
If she **hadn't found** out Rumpelstiltskin's name, she **would have had to** keep her promise and let him have her first baby.

Cinderella:
If the Fairy Godmother **hadn't appeared**, Cinderella **wouldn't have been able to** go to the ball.
If she **hadn't gone** to the ball, she **wouldn't have met** the Prince.
If she **hadn't lost** her slipper / shoe, the Prince **would** never **have found** her.
If the slipper **had fitted** one of the ugly sisters, the Prince **would have had to** marry her.

5 Writing to an English penfriend

1 **When** you **arrive**, my mother **will collect** you / **will pick** you up at the airport. (better: My mother **will** ... when you **arrive**.)
2 **When** you **are** with us / at our house, you**'ll be able to** have a rest / you **can** have a good rest (to start with / first of all). / ..., you**'ll** first **be able to** ...
3 **When I come** out of school / **get** home from school on Saturday, we**'ll be able to** / we **can** do something together.
4 **If** the weather's nice on Sunday, we**'ll go** swimming.
5 **If** you **don't mind** / If you **have** nothing against the idea, we **can** go to a disco in the evening.
6 **If** you **had come** two weeks ago, we **could have gone** to see / **would have been able to** go and see a great / fantastic Picasso exhibition.
7 **When I've read** 'Adrian Mole', I**'ll send** it back to you.
8 Or **do** you **want** to take it (back) with you **when** you **come** in June?
9 **When** / **If** you **look** at the photo, you**'ll notice** how Jens has grown / how tall Jens has got / grown.

Advanced Exercises

Other types of conditional sentences:
1 In this example, an imperative is used instead of the *will*-future. The meaning is more direct.
2 Here, *shouldn't* is an alternative to *don't*. It makes the condition seem less likely.
3 *Have* is used instead of *will have* here, and is part of a general statement not restricted to the future.
4 This is a mixture (in form and meaning) between Types II and III. The condition refers to the past, the consequence refers to the present.
5 Here, *were* (subjunctive form) is used instead of *was*. There is no change in meaning. (*If I were you* is a very common 'set' phrase).

7 Conditional Sentences

1 The language of advertising

Matching clauses:

1 – j; 2 – g; 3 – h; 4 – f; 5 – i; 6 – a; 7 – b; 8 – k; 9 – e; 10 – d; 11 – c

1 Slogan number one might be an advertisement for a bank or building society.
The second slogan could be from an advert for an expensive watch – or perhaps it's supposed to attract people who want to buy property / a house.
Slogan number three seems to be an advert for a lottery.
… 4 could be an advert for antiques / might be from an advert for a life insurance policy.
… 5 is supposed to attract people who want to organize their finances better.
… 6 might be from an advert for anything from Scotch whisky to holidays in China.
… 7 seems to be an advert for furniture sold by mail order.
… 8 is supposed to attract people who have plenty of money to spend (on luxuries). It might be from an advertisement for an expensive car.
… 9 seems to be from an advert for a marriage bureau / computer dating agency / lonely hearts club.
… 10 seems to be a special offer for something unusually cheap – or something good to eat. It might be from an advert for fitted kitchens – or a holiday cottage perhaps.
… 11 could be from an advert for a department store.

2 Most of the slogans are expressed with present tense and future or imperative forms. Only three are expressed with 'Type II' forms (past tense and conditional). The reason for this is that the advertisements want to offer real possibilities, and hope to influence readers to 'buy' what they are offering.

3 (free expression of own ideas)

2 Tough jobs

If I **was/were** an inner-city high-school teacher, and **was/were** frequently ill, I **would** probably **quit**.
If I **was/were** a miner, I **might drink** too much or use drugs. The best cure **would be** to limit my intake of alcohol – and quit the drugs.
If a junior doctor **suffers** from nail biting, or **has** a rapid pulse, he or she **should try** to exercise regularly and take refuge in his or her family and friends.

If you **should be** a journalist and develop an uncontrollable hunger for sweets, **try** to eat more sensibly.
If you **were** a waiter/waitress, you **might feel** irritable or bite your nails. Getting a massage **might help**.
If I **was/were** a secretary, I **might suffer** from lack of concentration – or I **might be** frequently ill. If that **happened**, I **would stand** up to my boss – **or** perhaps **change** my job. (etc.)

3 The 'ifs' of history

1 If Harold **had defeated** the Normans in 1066, French **wouldn't have had** such an important influence on the English language.
2 If Columbus **hadn't discovered** America, someone else **would have**.
3 Henry VIII **might not have broken** with Rome if the Pope **had agreed** to his divorce.
4 If the Great Armada **hadn't been defeated** in 1588, England **would have been invaded**.
5 If the American colonists **had been represented** in the English Parliament, the War of Independence **might not have taken** place.
6 If all the Indian tribes **had united** against the white man, they **might have been able to** prevent the whites from taking over the whole of their land.
7 If the economy of the Southern states of the USA **had not depended** on cotton, not so many slaves **would have been needed** – and so there **would be** fewer blacks in the USA today.
8 Britain **would not have been able to** found so many colonies if it /(she) **hadn't been** such a great sea power.
9 Slavery in the United States **might have continued** even longer if the Southern states **hadn't been defeated** in the Civil War.
10 The Americans **might not have landed** on the moon if they **had invested** less money in space research / if there **hadn't been** such intense competition with the Soviet Union.

Suggestions for other possible topics:
If Hitler hadn't come to power, …
If Germany hadn't been reunited in 1990, …
If the Channel Tunnel had been built fifty years earlier, …
If the automobile hadn't been invented, …

4 Fifteen

1 If Jane **wasn't** very careful what she said, her mother **would start** asking a lot of tiresome questions.

If she **knew** the boy, she **would know** something about his family / she **would be able to** look him up in the telephone book.
If she just **walked** past his house, he **might be** just **washing** the car **or mowing** the lawn.
If the boy's family **was** new in town, they **wouldn't be** in the telephone directory yet.
If he **didn't live** in Woodmont, he **might be** part of the school-bus crowd when school started.
If she **knew** where the place was where he worked, she **could walk** past about the time he might be through work.
If she **went** for a walk in the Nortons' neighbourhood, the neighbours **might begin** to wonder what she was doing.
If he **saw** her there, he **might stop** the truck **and talk** to her.
If she **said** she was going to Sandra's house, he **would give** her a lift.

2 If she **had been** a British girl ..., she **wouldn't have had** such long holidays, **or spent** so much of them ... (ll. 7–9): Type III
If only she **knew** the boy's name she **could look** him up ... (ll. 27–29): Type II
(*Note:* Clauses with *if only* express a wish and need not be followed by a main clause. Cf GG 76, GhE 214.2c)
... even if she **did,** he was probably so new in town that his family **would not be listed** .. (ll. 37–39): variant of Type II; the conditonal form is in the *that*-clause, with an extra main clause in the past tense
(*Note:* The clause with *even if* has both conditional and concessive meaning.)
If you **are** I'll give you a lift. (l. 66): Type I (variant with the present progressive in the *if*-clause: *are* = *are going to Sandra's house*)
If she **were babysitting** ... she **would be** sure to see him. (ll. 67–69): Type II (variant with the past progressive in the *if*-clause)

3 ll. 7–15: If she **had been** a British girl ... she **wouldn't have had** ... **or spent** ... And Stan **would not have been delivering** dog's meat ... (if he had been a British boy). In fact he **would not have been allowed** ... (etc.)
ll. 27–36: If only she **knew** the boy's name she **could look** him up ... **and** just **happen** to walk by his house, and he **might** just **happen** to be outside ... (if she walked by). She **would glance** at him ... And he **would look up** ... **and say** ... (if he happened to be outside) And she **would say** ... (if he spoke to her)
ll. 59–60: The neighbours **would begin** to wonder what she was doing (if she was walking up and down in front of the Norton's)
ll. 62–65 He **might happen** to drive by and see her ... (if she went for a stroll up the street where the Nortons lived next Friday afternoon)
He **would stop** the truck and say ... (if he happened to drive by)

4 The many conditionals show that Jane is unsure (about) what to do. She is imagining what she could do to meet the boy again, and thinking out the various possibilities. She has a logical way of thinking, and considers the problem from every side, weighing up all the advantages and disadvantages. All these thoughts seem to indicate that Jane is rather an introspective person, fond of day-dreaming, and full of romantic ideas. On the other hand, she seems quite practical, imagining exactly what consequences / results her various 'plans of action' might have. She also seems very determined, knows exactly what she wants, and will do all she can to get it.

5 Oder sie könnte ganz zufällig etwa um drei Uhr am Freitag nachmittag am Haus der Nortons vorbeigehen, wenn er vielleicht wieder gerade Cuthberts Futter bringen / liefern würde. Jane dachte darüber nach und entschied, daß der Plan sowohl Vorteile als auch Nachteile hatte. Sie könnte ohne weiteres in der Nachbarschaft der Nortons spazieren gehen, ohne fehl am Platz zu erscheinen / ohne dabei aufzufallen. Jedoch würde der Lieferwagen nicht genau um drei Uhr ankommen, und sie könnte schließlich nicht wie ein Streikposten vor dem Haus der Nortons auf- und abgehen. Die Nachbarn würden sich langsam fragen, was sie da machte. Trotzdem könnte es nicht schaden, am nächsten Freitagnachmittag einen gemütlichen Spaziergang ihre Straße entlang zu machen. Er könnte ja zufällig gerade vorbeifahren und sie sehen und denken, 'Hm, da ist ja das Mädchen, mit dem ich bei Nortons gesprochen habe.' Er würde den Lieferwagen anhalten und sagen, 'He, du. / Hallo. Gehst du zu Sandra? Wenn ja, dann nehme ich dich mit.' Und sie würde sagen ...

Note on the author:

Beverly Cleary (born in 1916) is a popular American author specializing in stories for children and young people. Although published first in 1956, 'Fifteen' is still read with interest on both sides of the Atlantic, as it deals with the 'universal' problems, hopes and fears associated with the process of growing up.

5 The greenhouse effect

If the pollution of the atmosphere **is not stopped,** the average temperature on/of the Earth **may/might/could rise** by between one and four degrees Celsius in the next fifty years. (Four degrees is roughly/just about/approximately the difference between temperatures now and (those) during the last ice age.) Terrible/Devastating/Enormous/Catastrophic changes in climate/climatic changes **would be** the result of such a development.

If present predictions **can be believed,** the world **should prepare** for a rise of sea level/for sea level to rise by about one metre some time during the 21st century. If the polar icecaps **melt** quickly enough, it **could be** two metres. And if the icesheet of the western Antarctic **should** also **melt** (although this is considered unlikely/improbable), sea level **might rise** by a further six metres. Bad news for people that live at sea level. Some scientists have been warning us for many years that the amount/level of carbon dioxide in the atmosphere is continuously rising/rising all the time. If (the) politicians **had listened** to them earlier, the situation **might not be** quite so bad now.

What can be done? One possibility **would be** to use nuclear power instead of fossil fuels. But if the countries of the world/earth **try** to replace fossil fuels by nuclear power, they **would have to** build between 3 and 16 nuclear power stations a week in/over the next 40 years.

An American scientist has calculated/has worked out that there is a simple method/way of changing/turning/converting part of the carbon dioxide in the atmosphere back into wood: an area the size of Australia **would** just/only **have to be planted** with sycamore trees/it **would** only **be** necessary to plant an area ... with sycamore trees.

8 Reported Speech

Basic Exercises

1 Waiting

... he asked her whether *she* **had made** *any coffee,* but she explained that *she* **thought** *he'd get a nice breakfast at the club.* She told him that *the car* **was** *there,* and that *she* **was** *(all) ready to go.* He wanted to know *where her luggage* **was,** and she reminded him that *it* **was** *at the airport.* ... he told her that *he* **was (just) going to get** *a few cigars.* ... telling her that *he* **would be** *right with her/back in a moment,* and instructing her **to get** *in the car.*

... she told the chauffeur **to hurry/to get** *going,* because *she* **was** *late.* ... Mr Foster ordered him **to hold** *it/***to stop** *a moment.* Mrs Foster wanted to know *what* **was** *wrong/what the matter* **was,** and he explained that *he* **had had** *a little present he* **(had) wanted** *her to take to Ellen/to their daughter.* He felt sure that *he* **had had** *it in his hand as/when he* **had come** *down.* His wife asked him *what sort of present it* **was,** and he explained to her *that it* **was** *a little box (which)* **was** *wrapped in white paper (which he* **had forgotten** *to give to her* **the day before.)**

... Mr Foster announced that he **had** probably **left** *it in his bedroom.* ... but his wife begged him **to leave** *it/***not to go** *back for it,* reminding him that *he* **could mail** *it.* ... and said *he* **was going to get** *it.* ... Mrs Foster was wondering *whether they* **could get** *to the airport in an hour.* ... she wondered *whether he* **had pushed** *it down there intentionally.*

Note on the author:

Roald Dahl (1916–90) was born in Wales, although both his parents were Norwegian. His short stories, which have been translated into many languages, have become international best-sellers, and a number of them have been dramatized for television under the heading of 'Tales of the Unexpected'. Dahl is also enormously popular with young readers. His bestselling children's books ('James and the Giant Peach', 'Charlie and the Chocolate Factory' and others) have made him well-known all over the world. 'Boy', an account of his early years, contains interesting descriptions of life at Repton, one of the big English public schools.

2 Disappointments and misunderstandings

1 'But you **told** me you **were going to give** her a record/she **didn't like** chocolates.'
2 '... you **told** me I **could collect** them today.'
3 'But when I rang up, you **said** I **could see** him straight away/immediately.'

4 '... I **thought** he **was** so clever/so good at school.'
5 '... You never **told** me you**'d got**/you **had** relations in Australia.'
6 '... I never even **knew** he **had** a girl-friend/he **was** engaged.'
7 '... I **thought** Toronto **was** in Canada.'
8 '... I thought he **was** (**training** to be) a vet.'

3 The case of the young woman named Sherlock Holmes

1   George Spencer *had told me* that a guy he **knew** ... **was going to marry** ... (ll. 2–4)
    I *said* this **was** nonsense, because there **isn't** any girl ... (ll. 4–5)
    He *said* I **didn't know** anything about it. (l. 5)
    I *said* it **was** dangerous to believe everything one **heard** ... (ll. 5–6)
    (I *thought* everybody **knew** that (ll. 9–10) can also be seen as reported speech)
    I **asked** him **to spell** out ... (ll. 11–12)
    ... he *said* he **didn't want** to (l. 12)
    ... I *mentioned* George Spencer and what he **had said** ... (ll. 12–13)

2 a 'Hi there, James! Have you heard the latest news about Harry Huff?'
     'Harry Huff? Who's he?'
     'A guy I know. He's going to get married.'
     'So what?'
     'You'll never guess the name of the girl he's going to marry. Sherlock Holmes! – Yes, believe me, that really **is** the girl's name.'
     'Are you crazy? You're talking a lot of nonsense, George! There isn't any girl called Sherlock Holmes. You know that as well as I do.'
     'You don't know anything about it, James. I tell you, Sherlock Holmes is the girl's name, you can say what you like.'
     'This guy's kidding you, George. In my opinion it's dangerous to believe everything you hear – and to go around repeating it. I've never heard anything so crazy.'
  b 'Hello? Could I speak to Mr Harry Huff, please?'
     'Speaking.'
     'I hope you'll excuse me for asking you this, Mr Huff, but I wonder if you could tell me the name of your fiancée.'
     'Now, wait a minute! What's the name of **my** fiancée got to do with **you**? Who **are** you, anyway?'
     'My name's Thurber. Sorry about this, Mr Huff, but could you just spell out her name, please?'
     'Are you crazy? I don't want to do that – and I don't see any reason why I should!'

'Well, it's like this, you see, Mr Huff. A friend of mine, George Spencer – you know him? – well, he told me your fiancée had a rather unusual name. He said she was called Sherlock Holmes! Well, as you can imagine, I find that pretty hard to believe. So I just thought I'd ring up and ask you ...'
'Mr Thurber! I really don't see that this is **any** of your business – but, if you must know, the name of the girl I am going to marry is Shirley – Shirley Combs. S-H-I-R-L-E-Y, C-O-M-B-S. Got that? Are you satisfied now?'
'Ah! **Now** I understand ...'
'Good**bye**, Mr Thurber!'

Note on the author:

James Thurber (1894–1961) was born in Columbus, Ohio. He was a journalist, and wrote humorous stories and fables, sketches and essays, many of which appeared in the 'New Yorker'. His best-known short story is probably 'The Secret Life of Walter Mitty' (1932), which is about a shy young husband's dreams of escape from the failures of his real life.

4 The giant ice-cream

... he saw an ice-cream stand with an advertisement/a model/a picture of an enormous ice-cream outside. He *thought* this **meant** that the ice-creams that **were sold** there **would/must be** giant ice-creams, just like the one outside. He *asked* his father **to stop and buy** him an ice-cream. So his father *said* he **would get** him one, and parked the car. They got out together, and went over to the ice-cream stand. Johnnie's father *asked* the man/woman behind the counter **to give** Johnnie an ice-cream/a large ice-cream, and when Johnnie got it, he *wondered* whether he **had been tricked.** He *couldn't understand* why it **was** so small! He started crying, and his father *asked* him what the matter **was.** When Johnnie told him, his father *explained* that the giant ice-cream **was** just an advertisement, and that in reality ice-creams **were** never as big as that. (He also *pointed out* that if there really **were** ice-creams that size, they **would melt** before you **had** a chance to eat them!) They got back in the car, and Johnnie began to eat his ice-cream, sadly *realizing* that things **aren't** always what they **seem.**

5 Missing

... Mark, their 15-year-old son, had gone out **that day,** as he often did on Saturdays. They explained that he had wanted to go to a football match, and

8 Reported Speech

that they had expected him back for tea **that afternoon**, but he hadn't come back. They hadn't wanted to call the police unnecessarily, but when he still hadn't appeared by nine o'clock **that night**, they had decided to ring up and report him missing.
At the beginning of November, we talked to Mrs Bassett. She said then that **the next/the following day** it would be three months since Mark had gone missing. She and her husband had no idea what had happened to him. It had been Mark's birthday **the week before**, she added, explaining that she had bought him a present as usual, hoping he would come home, but he still wasn't **there**.
Mrs Bassett said she and her husband were going to talk to the police again **the next/the following week**, but that the police had discovered nothing up to **then**. It was the uncertainty that was so difficult to bear, Mrs Bassett said. One day she thought to herself that perhaps **the next/the following day** at **that time** he would come walking in the door and everything would be all right. And another day she wondered if they would ever see him again.

6 Hedgehogs as pets?

Hedgehogs from Europe are the latest fashion in pets in North America at the moment. They are now being imported and have already appeared for sale in some pet shops in the USA.
Mr Rick Sisco, the owner of a pet shop in Fort Lauderdale, Florida, reported that travelling dealers **had offered** him young hedgehogs for $100/that he **had been offered** young hedgehogs for $100 by travelling dealers, but that they hadn't told him where the animals **came/had come** from. Mr Sisco didn't buy the hedgehogs. He said (that) he **couldn't/wasn't able to** give them the natural environment they **needed**.
In Canada, Mr Todd McBride, who wants to import hedgehogs and breed them as pets, said he **thought** (that) they **would appeal** as pets especially in rural areas. He emphasised/stressed that his application to import the hedgehogs **had been made** within Canadian law, which **laid/lays** down strict conditions for the import(ing) of/for importing animals.
Hedgehog lovers in (Great) Britain are against these exports. A spokesman for the British Hedgehog Preservation Society said (that) they **were** not against exporting hedgehogs to zoos, where they **could/can be bred**, but (that) they **didn't believe/think** (that) hedgehogs **were/are** suitable as pets, as they **liked/like** roaming/to roam, especially at night.

Advanced Exercises

1 Mr van Huyten makes an offer

'Mr Van Huyten and I had an interesting talk after the shop closed today. He started off by *asking* me whether I **enjoyed** my job at the works. Well, I *had to admit* that I **didn't/don't really** enjoy it as much now as I used to. And then he *asked* how I **liked** the work in the shop on Saturdays, so of course I *told him* how much I **enjoyed** it. Well, then he *asked* me whether I**'d** ever **thought** of doing that sort of work full time – but I *pointed out* to him that the money **wouldn't be** good enough for that.
Anyway, he *agreed* that it **wouldn't** normally **be**, unless you **had** an interest in the business. By now I *was beginning to wonder* what all this talk **was leading** to. He *started telling* me he **had** no relations, and that he **was getting** old and **needed** a full-time assistant. In the end he offered me a full-time job, with pay as good as I get at the works, and he more or less *said* that when he **retired**, he **wanted** to leave me the shop.
Well, as you can imagine, all this was a bit of a surprise! I *told him* I **liked** the idea, but I *said* I**'d like** to discuss it with you first.'

Note:
In a completely natural situation, Vic's parents would interrupt him occasionally with their own remarks, questions, etc. But interpolating these would make the exercise unnecessarily difficult. The corresponding passage in 'A Kind of Loving' might be of particular interest:

'Mr Van Huyten's offered me a full-time job at the shop,' I say, and watch the Old Lady's face.
'What did you say to that?' she says.
'I told him I'd think it over an' see what you an' me dad thought about it.'
'I think you're all right as you are,' the Old Lady says.
'What prospects is there in a shop?'
'Hold on a minute,' the Old Man says. 'It's not like a job in just any shop. Mr Van Huyten thinks a lot about our Victor. He nearly looks on him like his own lad ... Just what did he say, Victor? He didn't come out with it just like that, did he?'
'Oh, no; he went all round the houses, talking about how old he was and he has no relatives and he didn't want to divert me from my chosen course. You know how Mr Van Huyten talks.'
The Old Man nods. He's pretty sharp in a lot of ways, the Old Man, and he's on to this situation a sight quicker than the Old Lady is.

'Aye,' he says, 'he's a real gentleman all right.'
'But there's no money in being a shop assistant, Arthur,' the Old Lady says. 'Victor's nearly twenty-one an' he'll be due for a substantial rise then.'
'Oh, we talked about all that. He said the money would be all right.'
'D'ye fancy it, though, Victor?' the Old Man says. 'You know you allus wanted to be a draughtsman. You remember how chuff you were when you got that letter to say you could start at Whittacker's?'
'I was only sixteen then. I'm not sure I want that kind o' work now. It's not what Mr Van Huyten said makes me say that; it's been coming on for some time ...' I feel myself beginning to grin. 'I wouldn't mind, y'know. I rather fancy the idea.'

(From *A Kind of Loving* by Stan Barstow. Published by Michael Joseph Ltd., © 1960 by Stan Barstow)

Note on the author:

Born in Yorkshire in 1928, **Stan Barstow** was the son of a miner. He began his working life – like Vic Brown in 'A Kind of Loving' – as a draughtsman with an engineering firm. His writing career began with short stories, some of which were broadcast by the BBC. The success of 'A Kind of Loving' (1960), his first novel, which was later made into a film, made him decide to become a full-time writer.

2 The anonymous letter

1 **Direct speech:**
ll. 1–2: he thought, *I'm washing my hands ... of that damned letter.*
Indirect speech:
ll. 3–5: Ed ... had asked George ... if he'd seen anyone odd ... male or female.
ll. 6–7: Ed was sure George had asked ... the same question.
Inner monologue:
ll. 2–3: 'Who was writing ... probably.'
ll. 7–11: 'Was it someone ... even the clean-up men.
ll. 12–15: 'And perhaps ... as he was?'

2 **Direct speech:**
'Who **is** writing the letters? Someone who **lives** in **my** neighbourhood, probably.'
'**Is** it someone in **my** office? Inconceivable! Yet one never **knows, does** one? A poison-pen letter-writer **doesn't** necessarily **stare** at you, **wouldn't be** obviously an enemy. On the other hand, Anon's letters **seem** genuinely dim-witted, not like anyone at C. & D., even the clean-up men.'

'Perhaps **I'm** a little afraid, too. Someone **has singled me** out to write to. Or **am I** the only recipient? Are there other people in **my** neighbourhood just as annoyed as **I am?**'
Reported speech:
Ed wondered who **was writing** the letters. *He thought* it **was** probably someone who **lived** in **his** neighbourhood.
He wondered whether it **was** someone in **his** office, but *he thought* that **was** inconceivable, although one never **knew**. *He realized* that a poison-pen letter-writer **didn't** necessarily **stare** at you, **wouldn't be** obviously an enemy. But *he felt* that on the other hand, Anon's letters **seemed** genuinely dim-witted, not like anyone at C. & D., even the clean-up men.
Ed thought that perhaps **he was** a little afraid, too. *He supposed/realized* that someone **had singled him** out to write to. But then *he wondered* whether **he was** the only recipient, or whether there **were** other people in **his** neighbourhood just as annoyed as **he was.**

Differences:
In inner monologue questions are formed with the same word order as in direct speech, but the backshift of tenses is used as in reported speech (e.g. *is → was, lives → lived*) and the personal pronouns, possessive determiners etc. are changed as in reported speech (e.g. *my → his, I → he*).
There is an example of a question tag (*did one*, l. 8), which is not used in reported speech. Some sentences are unfinished (without a verb, or a subject, or a main clause), as in a person's actual thoughts (e.g. *Someone who lived in his neighbourhood, probably –* l. 3; *Inconceivable –* l. 7).
Apart from *Ed thought* in line 7, there are no introductory verbs.

3 The inner monologue makes Ed's thoughts and feelings especially vivid. One feels one can identify with what he is experiencing much more directly than if the author had used reported speech. One senses Ed's fear, and feels almost personally involved in his situation.

Note on the author:

Born in Forth Worth, Texas, in 1921, **Patricia Highsmith** decided to become a writer when she was still at school, editing the school magazine. Her first novel, 'Strangers on a Train', was filmed by Alfred Hitchcock. Since then she has written a large number of successful thrillers and short stories. 'A Dog's Ransom' appeared in 1972.

9 The Passive Voice

Basic Exercises

1 Biometric security?

1 **Rule 1:**
 ... that **will be designed** to recognize ... (ll. 4–5)
 If the computer ... **is shown** the correct personal data (l. 6–7) (cf. Rule 3)
 the door **will** automatically **be opened** (l. 7)
 but permission to enter **will not be given** to any 'unauthorized' person ... (ll. 7–8) (cf. Rule 3)
 Copies **can be made** ..., combinations locks **may be cracked** (ll. 9–10) (cf. Rule 5)
 the computerized cards that **are** sometimes **used** ... **are** frequently **lost or stolen** (ll. 10–11)
 buildings **could not be broken into** so easily (l. 12) (cf. Rules 4 and 5)
 biometric lock systems **are** already **being produced – and sold** (ll. 14–15) (cf. Rule 6)
 which **is** now **being introduced** (ll. 17–18) (cf. Rule 6)
 it **is not expected to be installed** ... (l. 19) (cf. Rule 5)
 biometric security systems **will be made** widespread **use of** (l. 20) (cf. Rule 4)
 Rule 2:
 But keys ... **could** eventually **be made** obsolete **by** a new kind of technology (ll. 1–3) (cf. Rule 5)
 ... a person's entry ... **will be controlled by** special computers (ll. 3–4)
 no more problems **would be caused by** 'forgetting your key' (l. 13)
 So far they **have been invested in** mainly **by** banks, ... (ll. 15–16) (cf. Rule 4)
 Rule 3:
 If *the computer* ... **is shown** the correct personal data (ll. 6–7) ('the computer' as a 'personal subject')
 but permission to enter **will not be given *to*** any 'unauthorized' person ... (ll. 7–8) (construction with *to* because the indirect object is very long)
 Rule 4:
 buildings **could not be broken *into*** so easily (l. 12)
 So far they **have been invested *in*** mainly by banks, ... (ll. 15–16)
 biometric security systems **will be made** widespread **use *of*** (l. 20) (This is a variation of Rule 4: the preposition is linked to the noun *use* in the phrase *to make use of*)
 Rule 5:
 But keys ... **could** eventually **be made** obsolete by a new kind of technology (ll. 2–3)
 Copies **can be made** ..., combinations locks **may be cracked** (ll. 9–10)
 buildings **could not** *be broken* **into** so easily (l. 12)
 it is **not expected *to be installed*** ... (l. 19) (passive infinitive after the passive form of *expect;* cf. GG 81, GhE 62)
 (*Note:* future and conditional forms like *will be designed, would be caused* can also be seen as examples of auxiliaries followed by passive infinitives)
 Rule 6:
 biometric lock systems *are* already *being* **produced – and sold** (ll. 14–15)
 which *is* now *being* **introduced** (ll. 17–18)

2 ... **is designed** to recognize the user's fingerprints or voice, so permission to enter the room or building **is given** only to that particular person. The advantages are that buildings **cannot be broken into** so easily, and locks **cannot be cracked.** So institutions that especially need security **can be protected** more effectively.

3 Schon seit vielen Jahrhunderten sind Schlüssel ein normaler / gewöhnlicher Bestandteil des täglichen Lebens. Aber Schlüssel und Kombinationsschlösser könnten über kurz oder lang durch eine neue Technologie – die Biometrie – überholt werden. Irgendwann in der Zukunft werden besondere Computer darüber wachen, ob eine Person einen Raum oder ein Gebäude betreten kann; diese Computer werden so programmiert sein, daß sie die persönlichen Merkmale eines Menschen, wie Fingerabdrücke oder die Stimme, erkennen können. Wenn dem Computer (oder der ‚biometrischen' Maschine) die richtigen ‚persönlichen Daten' gezeigt werden, wird sich die Tür automatisch öffnen; aber jeder ‚unbefugten' Person, die versucht die Maschine zu bedienen, wird der Eintritt verweigert werden.
Die Vorteile eines solchen Systems liegen auf der Hand. Von Schlüsseln kann man Kopien anfertigen, Kombinationsschlösser können geknackt werden, und die programmierten Karten, die manchmal für Hotelzimmer benutzt werden, gehen häufig verloren oder werden gestohlen. Biometrische Schlösser würden bedeuten, daß Einbrüche in Gebäude

erschwert würden, und natürlich würden keine Probleme mehr dadurch entstehen, daß man den Schlüssel vergessen hat/daß jemand seinen Schlüssel ...
In den USA werden biometrische Schloßsysteme schon hergestellt – und verkauft. Bisher haben sich hauptsächlich Banken, Forschungslabore und andere besonders sicherheitsorientierte Institutionen solche Anlagen angeschafft. Die gebräuchlichste Version des neuen Computers ist der ‚Fingerabdruck-Scanner', der zur Zeit zum Gebrauch in japanischen Haushalten eingeführt wird. Wegen seines hohen Preises ist nicht zu erwarten, daß er jetzt schon in vielen amerikanischen Häusern installiert wird, aber mit der Zeit werden biometrische Sicherheitssysteme wahrscheinlich weite Verbreitung finden.

2 Hallowe'en is being abused

1   **by** older people (l. 3)
    by a group of youngsters ... (ll. 13–14)
    by a lot of youngsters (l. 15)
    All these 'by-agents' are important because the meaning of the sentences would not be complete/clear without them.

2 a Complaints **have been made** by older people about children and teenagers abusing the custom of 'Hallowe'en'.
   b Flower-pots **have been kicked** over, and windows **have been smashed.** Fireworks **have** even **been thrown** through letterboxes. (More generally: Hidden threats **have been made;** cf. line 5)
   c If there is more trouble, action **will be taken** by the police. (The young people **will be taken** to the police-station/**punished** in some way).

3 a ... **were** never **heard of** ...
   b ... **is (being) dealt with** ...
   c ... **be made too much of.**
   d ... **be paid for.**
   e ... **are taken advantage of** ...
   f ... **to be looked into.**
   g ... **were looked after** ...

Background information:

Hallowe'en was originally an Irish custom – and the Irish brought it with them to America, where it has become a traditional 'party night'. The 'trick or treat?' idea (children going from house to house in fancy dress, with masks, etc., and demanding a 'treat' – usually sweets or chocolate) is comparatively 'new' in Britain, but in the USA it is a long-standing custom (cf. l. 4: 'this traditional American custom').

3 Facing up to vandalism

1 Pages **are/get torn** out of telephone books, so numbers **can't be looked up.** Windows in bus shelters **are** sometimes **broken,** and small children can **get hurt** if they fall on the pieces of broken glass. Trees sometimes **get damaged** – branches that **are broken off** might **get thrown** into nearby gardens/onto the road. Seats in parks **are** sometimes **broken, turned** over, **or thrown** into rivers, so they **cannot be used.** Lifts and escalators **are** often **damaged,** so stairs **have to be used** instead. Sometimes seats on buses or trains **get torn or cut** to pieces by hooligans, so they **can't be used.** Walls of public buildings **are** often **written on,** so they look unsightly. Gates and fences even **get broken or removed;** road signs **are** sometimes **damaged or knocked over** – or even **get painted over,** so they **can't be read.** (etc.)

2 Trees that **have been damaged** sometimes **have to be removed and replaced** by new ones/and new ones **have to be planted.**
   Lifts and escalators that **have been damaged have to be repaired.**
   Seats on trains that **have been cut to pieces have to be renewed.**
   Walls and buildings that **have been written on** often **have to be repainted.** (etc.)

3 (free expression of personal experience)

4 The new Noah

1 a Areas **have to be/are chosen** in which the animals are **to be found.** Then the animals **have to be caught and sent** to the zoos where they are **to be studied.**
   b He specialized in smaller animals because very little **is known** about them.
   c The Cameroons **were chosen** because it was a small country that **had not** yet **been influenced** by civilisation.
   d The reason is that their way of life **is affected** by civilisation, and they die out if they can't adapt to the new conditions that **are forced** on them.
   e African cooks and house-boys **had to be engaged,** and stores **had to be bought.** Hunting

9 The Passive Voice

permits **had to be obtained** from the Government, a lorry **had to be hired**, and all the food and equipment **had to be piled** into it.

2. a So little **is known** about the smaller …
   b Man **is** sometimes **influenced** by small animals more than by larger ones. / …**influenced** more by …
   c More damage **is done** every year by the brown rat than by any of the larger creatures. / Every year …

3. a … are to **be found** must **be chosen** carefully.
   b … can **be affected** … changes that may **be made** …
   c … may **be hunted** or **captured** / **captured** or **killed** …

4. **For zoos:**
Most animals in zoos **are looked after** well. A lot of money **is spent** on keeping them in a suitable environment.
Not all zoo animals **are locked up** in cages. Many of them **are kept** in quite natural surroundings. (etc.)
Against zoos:
It's cruel to keep animals in captivity, especially if they **are crowded** in small cages **or fed** with the wrong food.
I've heard that a lot of animals die while they **are being transported** to the zoos.
I think wild animals **should be left** in their natural surroundings. (etc.)

Note on the author:

Gerald Durrell (born in 1925) is a zoologist, whose TV series and books about animal life, including 'The Overloaded Ark' (1953), 'My Family and Other Animals' (1956) and 'The New Noah' (1955), have made him very popular. His elder brother, Lawrence Durrell (1912–1991), is well-known as a poet, novelist and travel writer.

5 Having it done

1. 'Yes, I really ought to **have it cut**.'
2. 'Why don't you **have it cut down / felled / removed?**'
3. 'Perhaps you could **have it repaired**.'
4. 'We **had it taken** by a professional photographer.'
5. 'I've got to **have a filling done / have a tooth pulled out / taken out**.'
6. '… if we **had had it done** professionally.'

Advanced Exercises

1 Other forms of the passive

1. 'an operation **being done**': passive form of the present participle
2. '**to have been sterilized**': passive form of the perfect infinitive
3. 'dislike **being prescribed**': passive form of the gerund
   'afraid of **being affected**': passive form of the gerund
4. 'in spite of **not having been stitched**': perfect form of the gerund, used in the passive
5. '**Having been given**': perfect form of the participle, used in the passive
   'while **being operated on**': passive form of the participle
6. 'the girl **being wheeled**': passive form of the participle

2 To wear or not to wear?

being seen – being influenced / to be influenced
have been threatened – to be closed – to have been closed – were sold
being forced / having been forced – being given
being worn – Having been brought up
are farmed – being put off – have … been worn – were informed – being brainwashed

3 An unusual friendship

1. Telephone calls **were made / had been made** at least a week in advance, and the exact time of Ruth's arrival **was** always **stated**. The time she was expected home **was** always **stated**, too.

2. Ruth **was looked after** too carefully **and protected** from every possible danger. She **wasn't allowed** to stay out long, and **was given** practically no freedom. Daisy, on the other hand, **was not watched over** so carefully, and **wasn't forced** to keep to strict arrangements. She **was encouraged** to run her own life.

3. The invitation, shyly **offered**, oddly **phrased**: The invitation, **which was / had been** shyly **offered** and oddly **phrased**
Daisy Brown **aged** fifteen (l. 1): Daisy Brown, **who was aged** fifteen
Ruth Perkin, also **aged** fifteen (l. 2): Ruth Perkin, **who was** also **aged** fifteen
Daisy, **accustomed** to … (l. 14): Daisy, **who was accustomed** to …

the restraints **imposed** on ... (l. 16): the restraints **that/which were imposed** on ...

4 The passive forms in lines 4–11 tend to create an impersonal atmosphere, as they are connected with the strict and formal way in which the Perkins deal with invitations. If the author had written, 'The Perkins had never asked anyone to their house' – or 'Mrs Perkins had arranged the visits/had talked to Mrs Brown on the telephone', the atmosphere would appear more personal.

Note on the author:

Nina Bawden was born in London in 1925. Her first novel, 'Who Calls the Tune', was published in 1952, and since then she has written many award-winning novels. 'The Ice House' was published in 1982. Many of her novels describe the way that emotional disturbances can threaten or destroy an otherwise comfortable existence. Nina Bawden has also written a number of books for children, the most successful of which is 'Carrie's War' (1973), which has been adapted for television.

4 The sense of smell

1 The sense of smell **is said to evoke** memories more quickly than our other senses.
2 Most people **are supposed/assumed to be** able to differentiate between about 4000 different smells.
3 People with especially sensitive noses **are** even **supposed to be** able to recognize 10,000 different smells!
4 Women **are thought/believed to be** more sensitive to smell than men.
5 A one-month-old baby/A baby of one month **is known to be** able to identify its/her/his mother by her smell.

6 Recently **it has been discovered** that mothers can recognize their children's T-shirts by their smell. / Recently mothers **were discovered to be** able to recognize ...
7 Up until the 19th century, body odour **was not considered** unpleasant. But **it remains to be seen** whether it will ever come back into fashion. / But whether it will ... fashion, **remains to be seen.**
8 In these days of deodorants and perfumes, such a development **is** hardly **to be expected!**

Grave humour

Optional exercise:
Explain the meaning of the inscriptions on the gravestones. What is funny about them? Do you think the humour is intended in all cases?

Unknown words could either be looked up in a dictionary, or the following explanations could be given:
grave: 1. serious; 2. hole in the ground for a dead body
to erect: to build, to put up
to drown: 1. to die in water because you can't breathe; 2. to make s.o. drown
Leith: port of Edinburgh in Scotland
affectionate: warm and friendly
to depart: to leave
to wind up (wind – wound – wound): 1. when a clock stops, you wind it up; 2. to bring to an end
wound up: very excited
sacred to the memory of: *zum Gedenken an*
discharge: *here:* the firing of a gun
orderly: an army officer's 'servant'
well done ...: quotation from St. Matthew, Chapter 25, Verse 25: 'Well done, thou good and faithful servant'
faithful: *treu*

10 Modal Auxiliaries

Basic Exercises

1 In human hands

1 'Money **can** buy many things' (l. 1) – expresses an ability

'Many things **have to** change' (l. 6) (substitute form of *must*) – expresses a necessity
'... nature **will not** tolerate lasting imbalances' (l. 13) – expresses a refusal
'... we **must** act decisively' (l. 16) – expresses a duty or necessity

10 Modal Auxiliaries

'... many people **are able to** continue' (l. 17) (substitute form of *can*) – expresses an ability

'... as well as they **should** be' (l. 20) – expresses a criticism (of the way 'things are going') – can also be seen as a moral obligation (i.e. 'we **should** be able to do something about it')

'... nothing **could** be further from the truth' (l. 21) – expresses a possibility

'... they **don't** all **have to** be done at once' (l. 25) (substitute form of *needn't*) – expresses that something is unnecessary

2 a can't; b won't; c must; d can't; e needn't; can.

3 a This means that we **must** use resources very carefully.
   b Human beings **can** solve this dilemma. / We **can** solve the dilemma ourselves.
   c When faced with a disaster that they **can't avoid / get away from.** / When they **have to** face a disaster ...
   d Others **have to / must** be done / organized by groups ...

4 We **ought not to** buy so many products that are designed to be thrown away after use.
People **could** save energy by spending their holidays nearer home instead of flying to places all over the world.
Parents **must** teach their children not to leave litter when they go out for a picnic or trip into the country.
People **should** make better use of the public transport available in their area, instead of always going everywhere by car.
Industrial waste **mustn't** be dumped in rivers or the sea; there **should** be stricter laws about the disposal of chemicals. (etc.)

2 The right thing so say

1 'Would you mind not smoking?' / 'Could you sit somewhere else, please, if you want to smoke?' / 'I'm afraid you **ought not to** smoke in here.'
2 '**Could / May / Can** I try them on, please?'
3 'You really **ought to / should / must** read this book.'
4 'You **ought not to** buy such expensive things!' / 'You **shouldn't have / ought not to have** spent so much!' / 'Thank you so much, but you really **needn't have** bought me anything.'
5 '**Could / Would** you move to one side a little, please?' / '**May** I go past, please?'
6 'I'm afraid this coffee's not very hot. **Could / Would** you take it back, please / bring me a fresh cup?'

7 'Be careful. The monkey **might** bite you.' / 'You **ought not to** put your hand into the cage like that.'
8 '**Could** you say that again, please?'

3 What can have happened?

1 'There **may / must** have been an accident.'
2 'We **ought to have / should have** rung up and booked tickets.'
3 'She **must have** forgotten to come.'
4 'He / She **may have** already gone to bed.'
5 'Someone **must have** thrown it away.' / 'I **ought to have** cut it out yesterday.'
6 'It / He / She **may have** been run over.'
7 'I **ought not to have** had so much cake!'

4 Doctor, doctor ...

1 shall / should; 2 was to; 3 are supposed to; 4 shall / should – ought to / should; 5 are supposed to / are said to – are to / ought to / should; 6 am to; 7 is said to / is supposed to; 8 ought to / should

5 Complaints

1 ('Can't you read?'). 'You **ought not to** smoke in here!' / 'You**'re not to** smoke in this library!'
2 (... at the supermarket) 'You **ought to** do all your shopping at the supermarket if you don't like my prices!' / 'Customers **are supposed to** realize that personal service will cost them a few pence extra!'

6 Unable to read

1 a ... he **wasn't able to** read a newspaper or comic book.
   b ... so that he **wouldn't have to** read anything / **wouldn't have to** do any reading.
   c ... it is important to **be able to** read and write properly.
   d ... what you **have to** do in case of emergency / if fire breaks out.
   e ... how many bottles he **ought to / must / is to** bring / deliver.

2 He **would** bandage his hand ... (l. 4)
... he **would** write huge words ... (l. 14)
He **would** get on the wrong bus ... (l. 16)

He used to could have been used instead.

3 a '... so I **wouldn't need to** fill in any forms.'
   b '... because I **didn't dare to** ask ...'

c '... I **needn't/don't need to** worry about things like that ...'
d '... but you **daren't** admit it ...'

4 He **must have hated** going to school.
He **ought to have** tried harder at school.
His parents **should have helped** him.
His teachers **should have taught** him to read properly.
The people at the dole office **may have realized** that he was trying to hide something.
His friends **must have known** what was wrong.
(etc.)

Advanced Exercises

1 Vice versa

1 'it **must have been done** somehow' (l. 11) – es muß irgendwie bewirkt worden sein
'what **could I have said** to start it?' (l. 13) – was könnte ich gesagt haben ...?
'though I **may have shrunk** into a little rascally boy' (l. 27) – obwohl ich mich in einen kleinen unartigen Jungen verwandelt haben mag
'You **shouldn't have wished.**' (l. 30) – Du hättest dir nichts wünschen sollen.

2 'What **should** I do at school ...?' – 'What **am I to** do? What **shall** I do? ... only suppose your sister ... **were to** come in ...!'
'I **wish** I was back again. I **wish** I was the man ... I **wish** all this had not happened.' – 'I **won't** be seen in this condition ...' – 'I **won't** have it.'

3 ‚Wage ja nicht die Klingel anzufassen!' schrie Paul. ‚Ich will in diesem Zustand von keinem Menschen gesehen werden./Ich will nicht, daß mich jemand ... sieht. Ich kann mir nicht vorstellen, was um alles in der Welt diesen Schurken von einem Onkel von dir veranlaßt haben könnte, so was Schreckliches mitzubringen! Ich habe noch nie in meinem Leben von einer solchen Situation gehört. Ich kann doch so nicht bleiben – es ist völlig undenkbar! Ich frag mich, ob es einen Sinn hätte, Dr Bustard zu rufen und ihn zu bitten, herzukommen; er könnte mir vielleicht etwas geben, was mich wiederherstellen könnte. Aber dann würde die ganze Nachbarschaft davon erfahren! – Ich würde zum Gespött der Stadt/von ganz London (werden). Keine Menschenseele darf je ahnen, daß so etwas passiert ist. Das mußt du doch selbst einsehen.'

4 Paul doesn't want to *look like a little boy*/doesn't want to *stay like this* because it means he won't be able to *go up to business as usual*/he may have to *go to Dick's school*/people might *laugh at him*. He thinks Dick ought to *give him the stone back* so that *no more damage can be done*.
But Dick feels *excited/pleased/amused* because the change in his father means he may have to *fit in with the role of a small boy*. He realizes that if the stone 'works' for him, he'll probably be able to *stay at home*/be allowed to *rule the household in his father's place*, while his father *will have to go to boarding-school and face all the unpleasant things that he, Dick, normally has to face*.

5 (free expression of personal opinion)

Note on the author:

Thomas Anstey Guthrie (1856–1934) wrote a number of humorous and magical stories, using **'F. Anstey'** as his pen-name. His most famous book, 'Vice Versa', published in 1882, was such a success that he was able to give up his work in the legal profession in order to write full-time.

2 Telecommuting: for stay-at-home workers

After the Second World War more and more people in Britain moved to the country, because they **were able to** lead a more attractive life there than in the cities. But as/since they naturally **did not want/wish** to give up their work, they **had to** go/travel into the city/into town every day – they became 'commuters'. Blocked/jammed roads/Traffic hold-ups, over-crowded trains, and the resulting loss of time have long put an end to their enjoyment of 'commuting'. For a growing number of people, 'telecommuting' – working for the firm from home – **could** be the solution to this problem/**might** solve this problem.
'Telecommuting' has many advantages – for women with small children who **want to** work at home, as well as for managers/executives/company directors, who **could** work more effectively if they no longer **had to** waste valuable time between their office/work and their home. Many employees **do not** actually **need to/have to** appear at the office every day; they **can/could** easily deal with/do part of their work at home.
In spite of the growing success of 'telecommuting', some people **are** still **said to** have reservations/there **are** still **said to** be reservations with some

people. 'How **am I to** know/How **should** I know whether my staff are doing any work/are actually working (at all)?' asks the traditional managing director/company director. The dangers **must not** be overlooked, of course. Human interactions are very important; people that always/constantly **have to** work alone/on their own **can/may** develop psychological problems. A further/Another danger is that the difference between home and work life **can** disappear/**can** be lost; people/ you either work too much, or they/you are more easily distracted at home, so that they/you work less as a 'telecommuter' than they/you used to/did before.

11 The Infinitive

Basic Exercises

1 Telling people what to do

1 We don't tell them **what they should wear**.
  ... **what they ought to eat**.
  ... **what time they must go** to bed or **get up**.
  ... **what risks they should take**.
  ... the basic human right to choose **what one wants to do**, and **when one wants to do** it.

2 Children should have the right to decide **what to do** in their free time.
  ... prefer to decide for themselves **when to sleep**.
  ... must be taught **how to tie** their own shoes.
  ... must tell patients **how often to take** their medicine.
  ... don't like being told **what to do**.

2 How they can help

3 If you don't know **how to cook** something/**what to cook**, a recipe will help you/might give you an idea.
4 A careers officer helps young people to decide **what career to choose**.
5 Commercials try to tell people **what products to use/to buy**.
6 If you set your alarm clock, you won't need anyone to tell you **when to get up**.
7 If you get lost in a big city, a police officer will tell you **which way to go**.
8 A tourist guide can advise people **what sights to see**.
9 A skiing instructor teaches people **how to ski**.

3 Psychological warfare

1 ... for a player **to score** ...
2 ... hopes **to score/to score** a goal now.
3 ... expect **him to get** a goal.
4 ... don't want **him to succeed**.
5 ... are pretending **to be frightened**.
6 They don't want **to be hit** ...
7 They would like **their team to win**.
8 ... is **to make Kevin nervous** and so to make **him miss (the shot)**.
9 ... want **to see Kevin score** a goal.
10 ... hopes **to save** ...
11 ... have managed **to make Kevin feel** unsure ...
12 ... wants **to take on** ...
13 He doesn't seem **to know** what **to do** ...

4 In and out of school

1 'Do you **want us to translate** the whole text?'
2 'I **would like you to choose** a poem you really like.'
3 '**It's important for the lab/laboratory to be closed** after the lesson (is over).'
4 'My parents **don't want me to study** art. They expect **me to take** over the family business.'
5 'I **want you to switch** off the radio/**to switch** the radio off. **It's impossible for you to (be able to) do** your homework with that noise (going on).'

5 Dr Watson at work

1 I **saw the naturalist pause** ... (l. 7)
  I **heard the key turn** ... (l. 11)
  I **saw him rejoin** his guest ... (l. 12–13)

2 He **watched Stapleton get up and go** out of the room, and he **saw Sir Henry fill** his glass **and lean** back in his chair with his cigar. He **heard a door open**, and then he **heard Stapleton come out and walk** along the gravel path. He **heard a key turn** in the door of the outhouse, and then he **noticed a**

11 The Infinitive

scuffling noise come from inside. A minute or two later he saw Stapleton go past him, and watched him go back into the house.

Note on the author:

Sir Arthur Conan Doyle (1859–1930) qualified as a doctor, and practised medicine until 1890. He wrote a number of historical novels, but it was the creation of Sherlock Holmes, the private detective, that made him world famous. Holmes and his friend Dr Watson, who shares rooms with him in Baker Street, London, have many adventures together. 'The Hound of the Baskervilles' (1902), of which there have been several popular film versions, is probably the most famous of his works.

6 Chief Joseph

1 For many years they **had allowed white explorers ... to travel** through their land. (ll. 3–5)
Chief Joseph never **permitted his people to sell** any land ... (ll. 5–6)
... the government wanted **to force the Nez Perce to give up** their land. (ll. 9–10)
This **forced him to realize** ... (l. 14)
Joseph **allowed his exhausted people to rest.** (l. 23)
... the Indians **were forced to surrender.** (l. 25)
Rather than **allowing the children to freeze** to death **and his people to starve** ... (ll. 25–27)
... and **allow the government to do** with his people what they wanted. (ll. 28–29)
The government of the US **told the Nez Perce to settle** ... in Oregon. (ll. 29–30)
... they **didn't permit Chief Joseph to stay** with his people. (ll. 31–32)
He **was ordered to live** on a resèrvation ... (l. 32)

2 Viele Jahre lang hatten sie weiße Forscher und Siedler durch ihr Land ziehen lassen, ohne sie je anzugreifen.
Häuptling Joseph ließ sein Volk nie Land an die Weißen verkaufen, weil er glaubte, daß das Land heilig sei.
Aber als im Jahre 1860 in den Bergen im Westen Idahos Gold gefunden wurde, wollte die Regierung die Nez Perce dazu bringen/zwingen/veranlassen, ihr Land aufzugeben.
Dies ließ ihn erkennen/zwang ihn einzusehen, daß er gegen die Weißen keine Chance haben würde.
Als sie schließlich die Bear Paw Mountains erreicht hatten, nur 30 Meilen von der kanadischen Grenze entfernt, ließ Joseph seine erschöpften Stammesbrüder (sich aus)ruhen.
Nachdem sie vier Tage lang standgehalten hatten, wurden die Indianer gezwungen, sich zu ergeben.
Lieber als die Kinder erfrieren und sein Volk verhungern zu lassen, entschloß sich Joseph, den Kampf aufzugeben und die Regierung mit seinem Volk tun zu lassen, was sie wollte.
Die Regierung der Vereinigten Staaten zwang die Nez Perce, sich in einer unfruchtbaren Reservation in Oregon anzusiedeln, aber sie erlaubte Häuptling Joseph nicht, bei seinem Volk zu bleiben. Er wurde gezwungen, in einer Reservation im Staate Washington zu wohnen/leben.

7 The 'let and make thriller'

A sudden noise **made** Bonner sit up in bed. The light of the electric clock **made** his wife's face look/seem ghostly. Bonner **let** her sleep on/carry on sleeping and went downstairs.
The wooden stairs **made** his steps/footsteps sound terribly loud. Fear/His fear **made** his heart beat faster. Had the dog **let** burglars in? The light of a torch in the sitting-room **made** Bonner stop breathing. He went to the telephone. His dry throat **made** his voice sound unnatural. '**Let** the burglar carry on,' said the policeman, 'and don't do anything that might **make** him turn nasty/violent.'
The policeman's voice **made** Bonner feel calmer. But what was that? A cry/scream **made** him jump ...

Advanced Exercises

1 Why do the British drive on the left?

1 a ... men carried **shields** in order to protect their hearts.
b **The sword** was used to attack enemies.
c The scabbard was used to hold **the sword.**
d ... difficult to mount a horse from **the right.**
e ... for a rider **to mount on the left.**
f ... decided to stand their horses **on the left** ...
g ... normal to keep **to the right.**
h True.

2 Das Herz befindet sich im linken Teil des Körpers (oder, genau gesagt, es scheint sich dort zu befinden). Deshalb wird in primitiveren Formen der Kriegsführung eine Art Schild benutzt, um die linke Körperseite zu schützen, wobei es der rechten Hand überlassen bleibt, die Angriffswaffe zu halten.

11 The Infinitive

Die normale Angriffswaffe war das Schwert, das in einer Scheide getragen wurde. Wenn nun das Schwert in der rechten Hand geführt werden sollte, so mußte (wohl) die Scheide links getragen werden. Mit einer links am Körper getragenen Scheide wurde es physikalisch unmöglich, ein Pferd von rechts/von der rechten Seite her zu besteigen, es sei denn, man wollte mit dem Gesicht zum Schwanz hin sitzen – was nicht üblich war. Aber wenn man von links aufsteigt/aufsitzt, so will man sein Pferd vermutlich auf der linken Straßenseite (stehen) haben, damit man vor dem Verkehr geschützt ist/ aus dem Verkehr heraus ist, wenn man in den Sattel steigt. Es ist/erscheint deshalb normal und richtig, sich links zu halten; die gegenteilige Gewohnheit (wie sie in einigen unzivilisierten/rückständigen Ländern praktiziert wird/die sich in ... eingebürgert hat) widerspricht völlig allen tief verwurzelten historischen Instinkten. Frei von willkürlichen Verkehrsregeln tendiert der normale Mensch nach links.

Note on the author:

The English author and historian **Cyril Northcote Parkinson** (born in 1909) is above all known for his 'discovery' of 'Parkinson's Law', which he satirically explains in his book of the same title (1957). It states that the more people are employed on a job, the less work gets done.

2 Another April

1 a ... he**'d walk** out into the snow and ice barefooted **and carry** wood in the house **and put** it on the fire. (ll. 4–6)
 ... **wouldn't bother** to put them on (l. 6)
 ... he **would cut** timber on the coldest day without socks on his feet (ll. 7–8)
 ... he**'d sweat** (l. 11)
 b I **had heard her say** ... (l. 4)
 I **heard her say** ... (l. 7)
 I **had heard her tell** ... (l. 10)
 c Now Mum **wouldn't let him go** out ... for she **wanted him to live** a long time (ll. 12–14)
 d ... he stopped **to examine** every little thing ... (ll. 15–16)
 Grandpa **would stand** ... **and hold** his face ... **and let the wind play** ... (ll. 18–20)
 ... he **was letting the wind cool** his face (l. 21)
 he stopped ... **to break** a tiny spray ... (ll. 29–30)
 e '... **it's funny to watch** Grandpa' (l. 33)
 f 'He**'s seen a lot of Aprils come and go**' (l. 34)

2 The little boy is too young **to understand** his grandfather's behaviour.
His mother tries **to tell** him more about her father/ **to explain** her feelings for him.
His grandfather examines everything in detail **in order to take** in the joys of nature as long as he is still alive.
The author manages **to describe** the old man very vividly.

Note on the author:

Born in Kentucky in 1907, **Jesse Stuart** has written novels, poems and stories. Although he came from a poor family in a country area where there was little chance of education, he went to University and later became an enthusiastic teacher back home in Kentucky. He is praised for his humorous and sympathetic descriptions of people and their lives in the Kentucky mountains.

3 Fast food in America

Fast food is meant for people who have no **time to cook** (a meal) themselves, or who are **too busy to sit** down comfortably and enjoy a long meal. Quite apart from that, they know exactly **what to expect** in fast food restaurants. They **expect the food** always **to look** the same, **to taste** the same, **and to cost** the same. But if you **would** really **like to know** what has made the fast food industry so successful, you only **need to ask** the next ten-year-old where he or she **would like to eat,** given the choice/if he or she had the choice. But how did all this begin?
In the 1940s Maurice and Richard McDonald were the owners of a successful drive-in restaurant in San Bernadino, California. They earned **enough** money **to be able to buy** themselves a new Cadillac every year. But in 1948 they **decided to close** their restaurant **in order to overhaul** it completely/for general overhauling. Paper plates were introduced **(in order) to replace** the dishes. The brothers showed their employees/staff **how to work** more efficiently. They **made them mass-produce** hamburgers. The new restaurant soon became **the place to go to**/the place everyone **wanted to go to**. For this was the first time that even families with low incomes **were able to afford to eat** out/**to go** to a restaurant.
The McDonald brothers were **the first to realize/ recognize** the chances/possibilities of fast food chain restaurants and hamburger factories. But they were not **the only ones to make** use of this idea.

In the 50s and 60s fast food restaurants **began to change** the face of American towns (and cities). Today the outskirts of towns/cities **seem to be** particularly dominated by fast food restaurants. Fast food restaurants **seem to prove** once again how **easy/simple** it is **to achieve/to realize** the American Dream / how **easy** it is **for the American Dream to come** true / how **easy** it is **to make the American Dream come** true: You only **need to know how to produce** a hamburger differently / **need to know** a different **way to produce** a hamburger – and you are a millionaire.

12 Gerunds

Basic Exercises

1 Life's risks

1 The risk **of dying** in a motor accident is smaller than the risk **of dying** in a climbing accident.
The chance of a policeman **being killed** on duty is about as great as the chance **of being killed** in a road accident.
People who smoke are in danger **of getting** cancer.
Driving a car is always a risk.
Mountain-climbing is a dangerous activity.
People should avoid **going** outside when air pollution is high.
If people want to reduce risks they should stop **breathing** altogether.
Although **smoking** can be risky, many people don't seem to worry **about dying** of cancer.

2 *a few suggestions, as examples:*
I'm fond **of climbing.** The idea **of looking** down from a height doesn't worry me. I've stopped **taking** part in really extreme tours though, because the risk **of having** an accident is fairly high.
I'm very interested **in riding.** There's always a danger **of hurting** yourself if you fall off your horse, but I don't mind **taking** that risk.

2 Parents and children

1 a ... against **Peter watching** TV ...
 b ... on **him coming** back home early.
 c ... about **him having** an accident.
 d ... for **them wanting** to protect him.
 e ... to **him seeing** too much of her.
 f ... on **him staying** at home as long as possible.

2 a ... mind **her coming** home late.
 b ... to **her staying** in bed / **having** breakfast late.
 c ... on **her acting** sensibly.

 d ... mind **her having** her own opinions.
 e ... about **her being** away from home.
 f ... prevent **her** (from) **organizing/running** her own life.

3 Rewards and punishments

1 ... between children, **as well as causing** big disappointments.
2 ... 'for fun', **without thinking** of financial rewards.
3 ... in a thing **by offering** a prize.
4 ... sums **for winning** a certain event.
5 But **in spite of being** worth so much money, these prizes ...
6 ... in the achievement **instead of considering** the prize important in itself.

Note on the author:

Born in Scotland, **Alexander Sutherland Neill** (1883–1973) became a teacher after taking his M.A. degree in English at Edinburgh University. He is best known for Summerhill, the school he founded in 1921 and which he once described as 'possibly the happiest school in the world'. The original idea was to make a school in which children should be allowed the freedom to be themselves. At Summerhill, now run by A. S. Neill's daughter, lessons are optional and all school rules are decided on democratically – with one vote for each pupil and each teacher. A. S. Neill wrote a number of books; 'Summerhill' (1962) contains most of his ideas on education and children's and parents' problems. He described himself as 'only a doer, not a profound thinker', but others have called him a genius.

4 Ego war on the road

1 War of the sexes **means fighting** between men and women.

12 Gerunds

Aggressiveness is **a feeling of wanting** to attack other people.
Patience **means not minding waiting or considering** other people.
Indecisiveness **is not being able to** make quick decisions/**means hesitating instead of deciding** quickly.
Over-cautiousness **is being** too careful.
Macho behaviour **means (men's) behaving** in an aggressive way.
Cutting in **is getting** in the way of another car, e.g. **by coming** out of a side road **or overtaking** too quickly.
Speeding **is driving** too fast.
Running costs are **the costs of driving** a car.

2 • Gerund as a subject:
   ... **drinking and driving** should be banned ... (l. 28)
   • Gerund as an object (without a preposition):
   Women, *asked to assess* their own driving, *cited* **having** patience and **displaying** ... (ll. 11–12)
   Examples ... *included:* **Cutting** in ...; **Speeding** ...; Dangerous **overtaking** ...; **Tooting** horn and **flashing** lights ...; **Refusing** to ... (ll. 18–23)
   ... they *enjoyed* **driving** (l. 37)
   ... try to *avoid* **driving** ... (l. 38)
   ... *dislike* motorway **driving** (l. 40)
   • Gerund after verb + preposition:
   ... they *worried about* **breaking** down ... (l. 16)
   ... they *were* regularly *criticised* ... *for* **their driving** (ll. 24–25)
   • Gerund after adjective + preposition:
   ... they are *terrified of* **breaking** down ... (l. 3)
   Men have to be *good at* ... **driving** (l. 7)
   ... were *afraid of* **breaking** down ... (l. 15)
   On **drinking and driving** they were *adamant* (l. 26) (emphatic word order, cf.: They were *adamant on* **drinking and driving**.)
   • Preposition + gerund as an adverbial phrase:
   ... they never drove **after drinking** (l. 29)

Note:
There are two types of gerund construction in the text that are not listed in the Basic Rules:
But their biggest fear was **breaking** down at night (ll. 13–14): gerund as a subject complement
... paid for all the **running** and repair *costs* ... (l. 35): gerund as an attribute to a noun, placed in front of the noun (cf.: the *costs of* **running** a car) (*raging* in line 1 is a present participle.)

3 (free expression of personal experience)

4 *a few suggestions, as examples:*
   I'm *tired of* **reading** articles of this type.
   Journalists should *stop* **writing** rubbish like this about the differences between men and women.
   Statistics like these are a good *way of* **informing** readers/**giving** the public the facts.
   Why should we be *afraid of* **admitting** that women think and behave differently from men?

Advanced Exercises

1 'A Life in the Day' of Debra McArthur

1 a ... insists on **having his own 'bathroom time'**.
      ... afraid of him **getting angry with her**. She admits **spending a long time in the bathroom**. ... a lot of time **doing his hair** in spite of **saying how old he is**. ... without **having any breakfast**.
   b She enjoys **going to school** but hates **being left behind/not being up to date with her work**. ... finds herself **giving it away or spending it on other people**. She dreams of **spending a lot on cosmetics** when she has enough money. Craig doesn't mind her **not wearing make-up**, but Debra is keen on **making an effort for him**. ... after **saying goodnight to Craig**. ... reason for her **getting up late in the mornings**.
   c She is fond of **looking after children**. ... thinking of **becoming a nanny**. ... succeeded **in dissuading her**. She dreams of **having children of her own** ... looking forward to **being pregnant/actually 'producing' the babies**. She is not crazy about **being a housewife**. ... about her **not knowing what career to choose**. ... concentrating on **getting good exam results**. ... dreams of **becoming rich and famous**.

2 (free expression of personal experience)

2 Brave New World

1 **Mustapha Mond:**
   ... occasions for **being heroic**.
   ... has succeeded in **conditioning everybody** ...
   no difficulty in **doing the 'right' thing**.
   ... no point in **resisting temptations**.
   ... solve them by **taking 'soma'**.
   ... why **being virtuous** is so easy ...
   ... without **making an effort**.

   The Savage:
   ... to bear **being bitten by mosquitoes** ... succeeded in **getting the 'Girl of Mátsaki'**.

... shows that **getting** something without **working** for it is too easy.
... won by **making an effort** are really worth **having**.
... a chance of **putting up with unpleasant things**
... prevented from **fighting to solve their problems**.
Getting rid of everything ... not worth **living**.

2 ll. 4–6: In einer richtig organisierten Gesellschaft wie der unseren hat niemand die Möglichkeit/Gelegenheit, edelmütig oder heldenhaft zu sein.
ll. 12–13: Die größtmögliche Sorgfalt wird darauf verwendet, zu verhindern, daß jemand einen anderen zu sehr liebt.
ll. 14–16: Man ist/wird so konditioniert/von seiner Erziehung geprägt, daß man gar nicht anders kann als das zu tun, was man tun sollte./... daß man einfach tun muß, was man tun sollte.

ll. 24–26: In der Vergangenheit konnte man (all) dies nur durch große Anstrengung und nach Jahren harter moralischer Schulung erreichen.

Note on the author:

Aldous Huxley (1894–1963) studied English at Oxford University. He soon became famous as a poet and a novelist. His most popular work is 'Brave New World', first published in 1932, a fable about a future world state in which social stability depends on a scientific system of 'castes': people are 'produced' scientifically to fall into certain categories ranging from the top intellectual to the simple worker, and they are conditioned from earliest childhood to accept their place in society. Aldous Huxley's elder brother, Julian Huxley, was famous as a natural scientist, writer and broadcaster.

13 Participles

Basic Exercises

1 The Great Plague

1 *List of participle constructions:*
a fever **known** as ... (l. 3)
A man **named** Samuel Pepys (l. 5)
a secret diary ..., **written** in shorthand (ll. 6–7)
... see ... houses **marked** ... (ll. 10–11)
and 'Lord have mercy on us' **writ** there (l. 12)
I find all the town ... **going** ... (l. 15)
the coaches and waggons **being** all full of ... (ll. 15–16)
people **going** into the country (ll. 16–17)
closed litters (l. 19)
a kind of hospital **known** as ... (ll. 19–20)
to see ... shops ... **shut** up (ll. 22–24)
... saw a naked child **being passed** ... (l. 25)
... he and his wife **being** now **shut** up ... (ll. 29–30)
... prevailed to have it **received** (l. 32)
..., **having** put it into new fresh clothes (l. 34)

a **closed** litters (from *to close*)
b I **find** all the town ... **going** ... (active meaning)/
saw a naked child **being passed** (passive form of the present participle – passive meaning)
... **see** houses **marked** .../to **see** ... shops **shut** up (cf. 1c; passive meaning)

c a fever **(which was) known** as ...
A man **(who was) named** Samuel Pepys
a secret diary ..., **(which was) written** in shorthand
... see ... houses **(which were) marked** ... (can also be seen as *see* + participle construction)
people **(who were) going** into the country
a kind of hospital **(which was) known** as ...
to see ... shops **(which were)** ... shut up (can also be seen as *see* + participle construction)
d ..., **having put** it into new fresh clothes:
... **when/after she/he had put** it into new fresh clothes
e ll. 15–17: I find all the town almost going out of town, **the coaches and waggons being** all full of people going into the country.
Ich entdecke, wie fast die ganze Stadt aus der Stadt zieht; alle Kutschen und Wagen sind voller Menschen, die aufs Land ziehen.
ll. 27–31: It was the child ..., and **he and his wife being now shut** up in despair ...
Es war das Kind eines Bürgers aus der Gracious Street, ein(es) Sattler(s), der alle seine übrigen an der Pest verstorbenen Kinder begraben hatte und der nun, da er selbst und seine Frau ohne Hoffnung auf ein Entkommen sich in ihrem Haus eingeschlossen hatten, nur noch wünschte, das Leben dieses kleinen Kindes zu retten.

13 Participles

2 *Picture 1:* ... You **can see people walking** along the street. You **can see two men carrying** a closed litter, and **another man pushing** a cart/wheelbarrow. **A dog can be seen running** behind him. **Smoke can be seen coming** out of the chimneys.
Picture 2: Here you **can see lots of people leaving** the City in boats/**lots of boats moving** along the Thames. You **can see three people standing** at the side of the river, looking at what is happening.
Picture 3: Here you **can see people carrying** coffins. **A woman can be seen carrying** a small coffin, probably with her own dead child inside. **One man can be seen lying** on the ground, perhaps ill himself, or already dead of the Plague.
Picture 4: In this picture you **can see people returning** to the City. **Two men** in the foreground **can be seen carrying** bags/bundles/sacks. You **can see people riding** back to London on horseback, and **carriages/waggons/carts can be seen moving** along.

2 My room

following (l. 1) – feeling (l. 2) – wanting (l. 3) – (too) impressed (l. 4) – extending (l. 7) – fitted (l. 7) – depressing (l. 9) – cream-painted (l. 12) – burning (l. 14) – leaving (l. 14) – hanging (l. 21) – chosen (l. 24) – meaning (l. 28)

Nun, während ich Frau Thompson in *mein* Zimmer folgte, bewegte ich mich in eine andere Welt hinein. ‚Es ist wunderbar,' sagte ich, wobei ich fühlte, wie unangemessen diese Worte waren und dennoch nicht zu beeindruckt erscheinen wollte; denn schließlich hatte ich ja bisher nicht in den Elendsvierteln gelebt. Ich schaute es mit ungläubigem Entzücken an; senkrecht gestreifte Tapeten in Beige und Silber, ein Erkerfenster, das sich fast über die ganze Länge des Zimmers erstreckte/das fast die ganze Länge des Zimmers einnahm, mit genau passenden Kissen, eine Liege, die wie eine Liege aussah und nicht wie ein Bett, das während des Tages bedrückend an Schlaf und Krankheit erinnert, zwei Sessel und eine Frisierkommode, ein Kleiderschrank und ein Schreibtisch – alles im gleichen hellen samtigen Holz. Auf dem cremefarbenen Bücherschrank stand eine Schale mit Anemonen, und im Kamin brannte ein Feuer, das einen aromatischen Duft ausströmte, ein wenig säuerlich und ein wenig nach Blumen riechend, einen Duft, den ich kannte aber nicht genau einordnen konnte.

Note on the author:

John Braine (1922–1986) is most famous for 'Room at the Top', his first novel, which appeared in 1957. The hero, Joe Lampton, ruthlessly works his way up the social ladder in a small Yorkshire town, marrying the daughter of a rich industrialist although he does not really love her. Its sequel, 'Life at the Top' (1962), describes Joe's later life and the feelings of disillusionment it brings. John Braine was able to devote all his time to writing after the success of 'Room at the Top'.

3 Get away from it all!

See the sun **rising/setting**/See a rainbow **building up/forming** on the horizon.
Watch the silvery moon **shining** on the sea.
Look at eagles **flying** over the Scottish hills.
Hear the birds **singing** in the trees ...
Listen to ... church bells **ringing** ...
Feel the soft wind **blowing** ...
Enjoy the **locally grown/home-cooked** specialities ...
Taste our **beautifully served,** delicious meals.
Try the **specially picked** fruit ...
Find ... flowers **beautifully arranged** for you ...
Be woken up by the aroma of **freshly made** coffee or ...
Rediscover the smell of an open fire **burning** ...
Be tempted by the homely smell of a **beautifully cooked** ... English breakfast.

4 Film of the week

... 'Piège', **produced in France in 1939.** ... **The story, drawn from a novel by William Irish,** depends on ... The cast, **including Franchot Tone, ...,** are particularly well chosen.
... who, **after quarelling/(after) having quarelled with his wife** ... **Arriving home/When arriving home,** he finds **his wife strangled,** and sees **the place crowded with police.** He is not afraid, **knowing he has an alibi.** ... But **not knowing her name,** ... People must have seen her **sitting with him** ....
... accidents, **the barman having been knocked down ... and killed,** and **the drummer ... having had the bad taste to get strangled.** ... **(having been) tried for murder and found guilty,** he begins ...... his secretary (Ella Raines), **convinced that he is innocent,** ...

Advanced Exercises

1 Heroic failures

1 *The surprised mugger* is the man who was / has been caught attacking and robbing someone (here: the old lady).
His forthcoming raid is the robbery he was / is planning.
Toughened glass is glass that has been specially strengthened so that it doesn't break easily.
A passing missionary is a missionary who was / is just passing by the scene of the crime.

2 a **Deciding to hire a pump,** he went out ... (l. 4): He decided to hire a pump, and went out ...
Returning indoors to make a phone call, he received ... (l. 5): When he returned indoors to make a phone call, he received ...
Having informed the police, hired a pump, sealed the leak and cleaned up his flat, Mr Heise felt ... (ll. 11–12): After he had informed the police, hired a pump, sealed ... and cleaned..., Mr Heise felt ...
Displaying an impressive versatility, he went ... (ll. 13–14): He displayed an impressive versatility when he went ...
Seeing, in May 1982, a robust man ..., he cried ... (ll. 18–20): When he saw, in May 1982, a robust man ..., he cried ...
... and leaped forward, **grabbing her assailant by the shoulders** (ll. 20–21): ... leaped forward, and grabbed her assailant by the shoulders
... Paul Lassis alerted the staff ... to his forthcoming raid ... **while driving up on the pavement outside** (ll. 25–27): Paul Lassis alerted the staff ... to his forthcoming raid ... while he was driving up on the pavement outside
With the entire staff watching, he reached out ... (l. 27): While the entire staff was / were watching, he reached out ...

These changes make the style more informal, and therefore less typical of written English.

b Als er sich während seines nächtlichen Spaziergangs plötzlich einem gewalttätigen Straßenraub gegenübersah, glaubte ein junger Arzt aus Brisbane, daß es für ihn nur eine Möglichkeit gäbe – nämlich einzugreifen. Als er im Mai des Jahres 1982 sah, wie ein kräftig gebauter Mann brutal mit einer alten Dame kämpfte, die auf der Straße um Hilfe rief, schrie er, ‚Hören Sie sofort auf!', sprang vorwärts und packte den Angreifer an den Schultern.

3 (free expression of personal experience)

Note on the author:

Stephen Pile (born in 1949) was a well-loved writer of a regular column in 'The Sunday Times'. His two humorous best-sellers, 'The Book of Heroic Failures' (1979) and 'The Return of Heroic Failures' (1988), were written, as he says himself, to 'sing the praises of the worst in every sphere, people who were so bad at their chosen endeavour that their names shine like beacons for future generations' – and as an antidote to our society's love of success.

2 Sorrow floats

1 ... On the plane **the father can be seen sleeping.** Lilly **watches / sees two ocean liners crossing** the Atlantic / **moving** in the darkness. At Frankfurt airport we **find them walking** to their connecting flight to Vienna. Frank **can be heard reading** the signs out loud, **and speaking** in German to everybody he sees. Later we **see them** leaving Frankfurt **and arriving** in Vienna / **going** on to Vienna in a smaller plane. We **see Frank being** sick.

2 'Knowing Egg' is different from the other participle constructions in that it does not refer to the subject of the main clause 'he' – and it has no subject of its own. Participles of this kind are sometimes called 'dangling participles' because they are not related to the subject of the sentence (cf. GhE 292 A 1). 'Knowing Egg, ...' means that it would be typical of him to be wide-awake during the flight, and not sleeping. (Anyone who knew Egg would imagine him being wide-awake ...)

3 Es ist zu unwahrscheinlich sich vorzustellen, daß Egg (gerade) schlief, obwohl es sich jeder wünschen würde; so wie Egg gestrickt war, war er bestimmt die ganze Zeit / Strecke hellwach – wobei Sorrow auf seinen Knien auf und ab hüpfte. Egg hatte sicher den Fensterplatz. (*Note:* would + the perfect infinitive here expresses what the speaker supposes to have happened because it would have been typical.) Und obwohl wir in die Stadt Freuds gezogen waren, muß ich sagen, daß Träume sehr stark überschätzt werden: Mein Traum von Mutters Tod war ungenau, und ich würde ihn nie wieder träumen. Sie schoß aus dem Himmel bis hinunter auf den Meeresboden, wobei ihr Sohn neben ihr schrie – Sorrow an seine Brust gedrückt.

Natürlich war es (auch) Sorrow, den die Rettungsflugzeuge sahen. Bei der Suche nach den gesunkenen Wrackteilen und dem Versuch, die ersten Trümmerstücke auf der grauen Wasseroberfläche zu entdecken, sah jemand einen Hund schwimmen.

4 The first part of the text is light-hearted in tone, and the detailed description of the journey is quite amusing. The news of the plane crash in the second part is very unexpected/shocking. The description of what (may have) happened to Mother and Egg is very striking/moving/well-expressed, and written in quite a different tone. The change has a rather depressing effect on the reader.

Note on the author:

Born at Exeter, New Hampshire, in 1942, **John Irving** is one of the USA's most original novelists. Even at school he longed to be a writer. A number of his books have become best-sellers, including 'The World According to Garp' (1978) and 'The Hotel New Hampshire' (1981), both of which have been made into successful films.

3 Journey of the Magi

1 The first verse of the poem contains a large number of participle constructions, many of them with subjects of their own. Some of the sentences have no real main clause, but consist only of participle constructions (e.g. 'And the camels **galled, ..., Lying** down in the melting snow.' / 'Then the camel men **cursing and grumbling** ...').
All these participle constructions suggest an atmosphere of restlessness, of hurry(ing), of 'being on the move', of a lot of different events happening over a fairly short period of time. They also seem to suggest movement and a feeling of travelling towards some kind of goal. A lot of the details described in this part are in fact 'accompanying circumstances', which are often expressed by means of participle constructions.
In the last part (ll. 32–43) the author mainly uses short, simple sentences. There are no subordinate clauses and only one participle construction (l. 42). The rhythm becomes slower. The style here reflects the speaker's conflicting thoughts about the meaning of his journey.
(*Note:* For a more detailed treatment of the poem cf. 'English and American Poetry' – 'Pupils Book' and 'Interpretations' – Klettbooks 5064 and 50643)

2 ... The men hated the journey, and some of them ran away. Sometimes the fires went out, and they found nowhere to spend the night. The places they travelled through were unpleasant and the people they met were unfriendly. Prices were high too. In the end they decided to travel through the night and sleep little. All the time they felt that what they were doing was foolish, and that the journey was pointless.

Note on the author:

One of the most influential poets of the 20th century, **Thomas Stearns Eliot** (1888–1965) was born in St Louis, Missouri, and educated at Harvard, the Sorbonne and Oxford University. He then settled in England and became a British subject and a member of the Church of England in 1927. By this time he was already recognized as a figure of great cultural authority. Among his most famous poems are 'The Love Song of J. Alfred Prufrock' (1915), 'The Waste Land' (1922) and 'The Journey of the Magi' (1927). His popular collection of verse for children, 'Old Possum's Book of Practical Cats' (1939), provided the lyrics for the highly successful Andrew Lloyd Webber musical 'Cats', which was first performed in 1981. Eliot was also a dramatist and a literary critic. He was awarded the Nobel Prize for Literature in 1948.

14 Non-finite Verb Forms: Mixed Exercises

Basic Exercises

1 The boxing match

spending – beat/beating – seeing – fight – saying – become

staring – to look – (to) frighten – sound dancing/dance – to avoid – throw – hit – to send (= um ... zu schicken; also possible: 'stopped the fight, sending ...' = indem er ... schickte) – counting/to count – holding/hold – go – drop – crash

yelling / to yell – shout / shouting – using – tap – standing
insulting – to annoy – to look – shouting – raise – going

2 School's over: What now?

1 'I'm looking forward to **earning** some money at last.'
2 'After/When I leave school, I want **to study** architecture. I'm already dreaming of **designing** my own house / a house of my own.'
3 'I've thought of / been thinking of **going** to America for a few months and **working** there.'
4 'I'd quite / rather like **to work** for a tourist agency. But I wouldn't be interested in **sitting** in an office all day.'
5 'I think you / one ought **to do** something really worthwhile instead of always only **thinking** of (the) money.'
6 'My parents have always wanted me **to work** in the family business. I don't know how **to say** no without **disappointing** them. I' afraid of **telling** them the truth – but on the other hand, it's no use / no good **starting** something that doesn't interest me at all.'

3 Danger, mountains!

... people **being killed** while **walking** ...
... makes tourists **think** ... used to **walking** ... find themselves **stranded** ... fail **to take** ... before **setting off**.
... people **wearing** ... try **to climb** mountains without **realizing** ... suitable **to protect** ... remember **to check** ... forget **to take** ... and **(to) leave** ...
... how **to make** ... visitors **to be** aware ... against **putting up** ... clearly **marked** paths ... hills **to be spoilt** ... people **believing** ... against **making** things **seem** easier ...

4 Pilots win top bravery award for drilling rig rescue

... for **saving** 51 workers ... (l. 3) ... **landing** on the rig ... (l. 6) ... skill in **saving** the workers ... (l. 9)
... while **being moved** (l. 17)
... the first **to arrive** ... (l. 21) ... difficulty in **flying** ... (l. 23) ... **flying** ten **relieved** crewmen ... (l. 26) ... managed **to land** ... (l. 30) ... were able **to escape** ... (l. 31)
... saw the rig lights **go out**. **Knowing** that ... (l. 34–35) ... decided **to try** ... (l. 36) ... searchlights **shining** ... (l. 38) ... 11 men **crawling** on hands and knees **to reach** ... (ll. 41–42)

Captain Gregg, **speaking** in America (l. 45) ...
four guys **doing** a job ... (l. 46) ... could be **saved** (l. 50)

Advanced Exercises

1 Help us save the dolphins

1 *Panic-stricken* means that they are so frightened that they don't know what to do.
The ensuing confusion is the moments of chaos following the closing of the net / after the net closes.
Deprived of air means that they are not able to breathe.
Bodyparts ripped away means that parts of the dolphins' bodies have been torn off.
Alternative fishing techniques are other / different methods of fishing / of catching fish.

2 a 'hope of **catching**' (l. 7): gerund after a noun + preposition
'without **hurting**' (l. 26): gerund after a preposition, as an adverbial phrase
'by **acting** today' (l. 28): gerund after a preposition, as an adverbial phrase
'stop them **butchering**' (l. 29): gerund (with a subject of its own) after the verb 'to stop'
b 'set out **to take** advantage' (l. 4–5)
'**To campaign** effectively, we need ...' (l. 28)
c These participle constructions are used instead of relative clauses.
'in an area **which/that is called** ...'; 'the sharks **which/that are attracted** by the carnage **which/that is taking place**'

3 (easily) spotted; drowned; tangled; terrified; deprived (of air); (bodyparts) ripped (away); maimed; injured.
Most of these participles refer to the way the dolphins are treated by the tuna fishermen, and show the results of their fishing techniques. These participles emphasize what is **done** to the innocent dolphins. They are passive victims, helpless and unable to escape. So the reader feels urged to do what he or she can to help.

4 The World Wildlife Fund tries to help endangered animals and birds by protecting their natural environment.
People's support will enable Unicef to help and protect children in many different parts of the world.
(etc.)

14 Non-finite Verb Forms: Mixed Exercises

2 Some animals are more equal than others

1 **Gerunds:**
neighing (l. 3): used as a noun (here: as subject)
used to **supporting** (l. 9): after verb + preposition
baying; crowing (l. 15): used as nouns
the habit ... of never **complaining,** never **criticizing** (l. 23–24): after noun + preposition
bleating (l. 26): used as a noun
without **stopping** (l. 28); without **saying** (l. 32): after preposition, as adverbial phrases
lettering (l. 35): used as a noun

Infinitives:
watched the ... pigs **march** (l. 20): after a verb of perception + object
the chance **to utter** (l. 29): after a noun
they used **to be** (l. 38): after the auxiliary verb *used to*
consented **to break** (l. 40): after a verb

Present participles:
a pig **walking** ... (l. 7): instead of a relative clause
pigs, all **walking** ... (l. 11): instead of a relative clause
casting haughty glances (l. 16): instead of a main clause, to express accompanying circumstances
with his dogs **gambolling** round him (l. 17): with a subject of its own and introduced by *with;* instead of a main clause, to express accompanying circumstances
huddling together (l. 19): instead of a main clause, to express accompanying circumstances
Benjamin felt a nose **nuzzling** ... (l. 31): after a verb of perception + object
they stood **gazing** (l. 35): after a verb describing a position

Past participles:
the **terrified** neighing of a horse (l. 3): used as an adjective
Startled, ... (l. 4): instead of an adverbial clause or a main clause (As they were startled, the animals .../The animals were startled and ...)
Amazed, terrified, ... (l. 19): instead of a main clause, to express accompanying circumstances
(Note: startled, amazed and terrified can also be seen as adjectives.)
the habit, **developed** through long years, ... (l. 23): instead of a relative clause
the **tarred** wall (l. 35): used as an adjective

2 a These past participles are used to describe the animals' behaviour and their reaction to what they see and hear / to the new developments on 'Animal Farm'.
b They describe the sounds the animals make.
c *used to supporting* (adjective + preposition + gerund) describes a habit; *used to be* (auxiliary + infinitive) expresses a state in the past.
Ein wenig unbeholfen, als ob er es nicht ganz gewöhnt wäre, seinen beträchtlichen Körperumfang auf den Beinen zu halten, aber vollkommen im Gleichgewicht, schlenderte er über den Hof.
Sind die Sieben Gebote immer noch dieselben wie früher? / Lauten die ... immer noch gleich / so wie früher?
d The infinitive is used to describe a completed action; the participle describes an action in progress.

3 Und schließlich hörte man ein furchtbares Hundegebell und das schrille Krähen des jungen schwarzen Hahnes, und dann kam Napoleon selbst heraus, majestätisch aufrecht, hochmütige Blicke nach allen Seiten um sich werfend, während seine Hunde um ihn herumtollten.
Er trug eine Peitsche in der Pfote.
Es herrschte (eine) Todesstille. Verblüfft, voller Angst, dicht zusammengedrängt, beobachteten die Tiere, wie die lange Reihe der Schweine um den Hof herummarschierte. Es schien, als ob die Welt auf dem Kopf stünde.

4 ... Then we **see the animals rush** into the yard. In the yard, we **see Squealer walking** on his hind legs. A moment later, we **see the other pigs come** out of the farmhouse, also on their hind legs. Then we **hear the dogs bark(ing) and the cockerel crow(ing)** and we **see Napoleon come** out with his dogs.
We **see the animals huddling** together, terrified. Then we **hear the sheep bleating:** 'Four legs good, two legs *better*!' Soon we **see the pigs disappear** back into the farmhouse.
In the next part of the scene, we **see Benjamin and Clover go(ing)** to the big barn, and we **hear Clover ask** Benjamin whether the Seven Commandments are still the **same.** Finally we **hear Benjamin read** out the single Commandment: 'All animals are equal ...'

5 a They **seem to play** the role of leaders, and they **seem to take / to have taken** over the role of the original human masters.
b They **try to walk** on their hind legs because they **want to imitate** human beings.

c When they **see the pigs march(ing)** on two legs, they feel **worried** and **frightened**.
d The whip means that Napoleon **intends/plans/wants to rule** over the other animals as a dictator. He **plans to punish** any animals that might **try to rebel** against his leadership.
e They **seem to influence** the other animals' behaviour **by preventing** them **from voicing** their complaints / **by making** a loud noise just at the moment when the animals **feel like protesting**.
f It means that the pigs have **decided to put** themselves in a position of superiority / of authority over the other animals.

Note on the author:

Eric Arthur Blair (1903–50), born in Bengal, but brought up and educated in England, wrote under the pen-name of **'George Orwell'**. He was a successful journalist and essay writer, but he is best known for his novels. The two most famous ones are 'Animal Farm' (1945), a satirical fable, and 'Nineteen Eighty-Four' (1949), a nightmarish story of one man's unsuccessful struggle against a totalitarian state. Orwell has been especially praised for his straightforward, conversational style, which makes his work extremely readable.

3 Traveling through the dark

1 a It is best **to roll/push** them off the road **(in order) to avoid risking/causing** another accident.
b **By touching** the doe, he discovers that she has an unborn fawn inside her/her belly.
c It means that the fawn **is waiting for the time of its birth to arrive** – but that this time will never come because its mother is now dead.
d He feels that he is alone with nature, and that only the wilderness can understand his thoughts / that the wilderness **is waiting for him to come** to the decision he has to make.
e It could mean the speaker's hesitation, the moment when he wonders **how to act/what to do/whether to try** to save the fawn or not.

2 a The doe is cold, stiff and motionless. The car is warm ('glow of the tail-light', 'warm exhaust') and **seems to be** alive ('purred the steady engine'). There **seems to be** a contrast between life and death, between stillness and motion. The animal, which would normally symbolize life, is now dead, while the car, an inanimate object, **seems to be** 'alive'.
b He wonders **whether to try to save** the unborn fawn somehow. But there **seems to be no way of doing** this, and so – in the interests of safety – he **decides to push** the dead deer over the edge of the road.
c 'Traveling through the dark' at first **seems to mean** only the journey by car at night. It **could** also **refer** to the 'journey' of the fawn through the various stages of development before birth, in the darkness of its mother's belly. Thirdly, it **could be interpreted** as the speaker's confrontation with a problem he feels he does not know / is unsure **how to solve.**

Note on the author:

Born in Hutchington, Kansas, in 1914, **William Stafford** studied at the University of Kansas and at Iowa State University. Later he became professor of literature at Lewis and Clark College in Portland, Oregon. He is known for the straightforward, communicative style of his poetry.

15 Verbs and their Objects

Basic Exercises

1 Bits and pieces

1 The explorers described the details of their journey to (the) waiting reporters.
2 The farmer sold a large area of land to the council / sold the council a large area of land.
3 The film director promised the young film star a part in the new film.
4 The tourist asked a traffic warden the way to the station.
5 The demonstrators handed leaflets to the crowds in the street.
6 The loudspeaker announced to the impatient passengers the news that the flight was delayed.

15 Verbs and their Objects

7 The neighbours reported the burglary to the police.
8 (see example)

2 The do-it-yourself cottage

... left him quite a sum of money. (l. 2) ... buy his family an old cottage ... (l. 5) ... meant a lot to him and his wife. (ll. 6–7)
... gave the question a lot of thought (l. 8) ... announcing his decision to his family. (l. 9) ... mentioned his idea to their friends (l. 11) ... offered him their help and advice. (ll. 12–13)
... found a dream cottage for his family/his family a dream cottage (ll. 14–15) ... gave them planning permission. (ll. 17–18)
... booked rooms in the local inn for everybody/ everybody rooms ... (ll. 19–20) ... to offer the Turners as much time as they could (ll. 21–22) ... promising themselves a little holiday (ll. 22–23) ... sent building materials to Mr Turner and his helpers (ll. 24–25) ... gave them help ... (l. 25)
It took them a long time (l. 27) ... cost the Turners very much. (l. 28) ... offered his friends free use of the cottage (ll. 30–31)

3 At the tourist information centre

1 Could you reserve/book me a hotel room/a hotel room for me, please?
2 The way to the old castle is rather complicated. I'm afraid I can't describe it to you very well. I'd better give you a town plan/a plan/map of the town.
3 The tour of the city/guided tour/round trip is really an experience. We recommend it to all our guests/visitors.
4 I don't quite understand what you mean. Could you explain it to me again?
5 I can offer you (some) cheap tickets for Friday. If you buy them at the theatre box office, they'll cost you quite a lot more.

4 How much to tip?

1 unlocked **my room for me** (l. 3): type *buy* – though with *to unlock* the construction with *for* is the only one possible
telling **me the names of all the New York radio stations** (ll. 8–9): type *give*
handing over **money to people** (l. 25): type *give*
what you should tip **a person** (l. 27): type *ask*
giving **somebody half a dollar** (l. 29): type *give*
give **me thirty-five cents** back (l. 31): type *give*
tipped **the driver ten cents** (l. 32–33): type *ask*

gave **the driver my dime** (l. 34–35): type *give*
handed **him a Canadian dime** type *give* (l. 37–38)

2 He **unlocked her room for her, showed her the hot and cold taps (explained to her how they worked), and switched the radio on for her.** He even **told her the names of all the New York radio stations.** He got angry because she **didn't tip him anything/didn't give him a tip.**

3 When Esther took her first taxi in New York, she thought she was doing the right thing by **tipping the driver exactly ten per cent of the fare.** But the driver looked at the dime as if she **had given him Canadian money** by mistake. In actual fact, he had been expecting her **to give him a bigger tip.**

4 The receptionist will **give you your room key.**
The porter will **carry your luggage** to your room **for you.**
A waiter will **bring you your meals/show you the menu.**
The barman will **sell you drinks.**
The chambermaid will **make your bed for you.**
(etc.)

5 (free expression of personal opinion)

Note on the author:

Born and brought up in the United States, **Sylvia Plath** (1932–1963) completed her studies at Cambridge University. She married the English poet Ted Hughes in 1956, and they lived in England from 1959 until her death by suicide in 1963. She is best-known as a poet; 'The Bell Jar' (1963), her only novel, was published only a few weeks before she died.

Advanced Exercises

1 What the British think of the monarchy

A lot of people considered the royal family hard-working.
16% regarded them as extravagant.
They were looked upon as highly respected by over half the people interviewed.
Only about a third called them intelligent.
Some people thought them in touch with ordinary people.
Not many people thought of them as a family just like any other.

A few people found the royal family important to their lives. (etc.)
(+ free expression of opinion)

2 Innocent or guilty

pronounced the accused man **(not) guilty**. ... considered the verdict **fair/right/just**. ... declared the witnesses **fools/unreliable/unfair/liars/prejudiced**. ... called the judge **unfair/inhuman/crazy/incompetent/a fool/a madman**. ... thought the judge's decision **right/correct/fair/wrong/unfair**. ... found her husband **unbearable/difficult to live with/crazy/an ideal partner/a wonderful man**. ... which she looked upon as **just/right/ridiculous/absurd** ... made **her happy/a happy woman/very unhappy/bitterly disappointed**.

3 Historical facts

1 ... was crowned **Queen of England**.
2 ... to be elected **Prime Minister**.
3 ... officially made **free** ... considered them **equal**.
4 ... is regarded **as one of the most important documents ever written**.
5 ... was looked upon **as men's business/as something that only concerned men**.
6 ... was thought of **as quite normal**. ... was finally made **illegal** ...

4 Melting pot or mixed salad?

1 Teachers ... *are giving* **more ... attention to the problem** ... (ll. 1–2): two objects
... statistics *show* **us a very different picture** ... (ll. 4–5): two objects
... a headmaster's methods *cost* **him his job**. (ll. 8–9): two objects
... *to give* **special treatment to Muslim children**. (ll. 9–10): two objects
... he *described* **his standpoint to the ... authority**. (ll. 11–12): two objects
I *consider* **a melting pot** *more realistic*... (ll. 12–13): object complement
... *to make* **them** *British*. (l. 14): object complement
... *teach* **them the English language**, *explain* **English institutions to them** ... *offer* **them lessons** ... (ll. 14–17): two objects
... it *makes* **the children** *more aware* ... (ll. 18–19): object complement
... *finds* **such attitudes** *very worrying*. (ll. 20–21): object complement

... *regards* **racism** *as the major problem* ... (ll. 21–22): object complement
... *offer* **courses ... to teachers** ... (ll. 23–24): two objects
... *ways to explain* **to young people what racism can lead to**. (ll. 26–27): two objects
... *describe* **to pupils the effects of slavery** ... (ll. 28–29): two objects
... *devote* **teaching time to Muslim festivals** ... (ll. 30–31): two objects
... **children** could ... *be called Janet and John ... Hanif and Aruna*. (ll. 32–34): verb with object + object complement in the passive (cf.: They can *call* **children** ... *Hanif and Aruna*.)

2 a He lost his job because he did not want to *give* **special treatment to Muslim children**. He *considered* it *important to make* **Asian children** *British*. He did not *regard* **a 'mixed salad'** *as the solution to the problems of living together*. He believed multi-culturalism would *make* **Asian children** *more aware of the differences between themselves and the British*.
   b It *considers* **racism** *as a major problem,* and wants to *give* **teachers special courses in multi-culturalism**.
   c They could *devote* **more time to Muslim traditions**, for example, or they could *explain* **to children the effects of slavery**.

3 In dieser Stadt im Norden brachten die Methoden eines Schuldirektors ihn/diesen um seinen Arbeitsplatz. Er hatte sich geweigert, moslemischen Schülern eine besondere Behandlung zukommen zu lassen. Gegenüber der örtlichen Schulbehörde beschrieb er seinen Standpunkt auf folgende Weise: ‚Was wichtig ist, ist die Integration. Ich halte einen Schmelztiegel/ein Zusammenschmelzen der Rassen für realistischer als einen gemischten Salat. Unsere Aufgabe ist es, sie zu Briten zu machen. Wir müssen sie die englische Sprache lehren, ihnen englische Institutionen erklären und ihnen selbst/sogar christlichen Religionsunterricht anbieten. Eine multikulturelle Politik wird nie funktionieren, weil sie den Kindern ihre Andersartigkeit/die Unterschiede zwischen sich und den anderen noch stärker bewußtmacht.'

4 (free expression of personal opinion)
Useful phrases containing structures to be practised:
I find his attitude ...
I regard this kind of standpoint as ...
I think it right/wrong/sensible/unwise to give .../ to teach ...
I find the idea of a melting pot ...

16 Relative Clauses

Note:
In conversational English, the construction with object and object complement is often avoided when an opinion is stated, and a *that*-clause is used instead. Examples:
Formal: I **regard** your decision **as wise.**
We **do not think it important** ...
Informal: I **think** your decision **is wise.**
We **don't think it's important** ...
The alternative construction with *to be* is also very common in formal English:
I **consider** racism **to be** one of the greatest problems we face today.
Until recently, a good education **was thought to be** a guarantee of a good job.

5 Laurence Olivier: 1907–1989 – virtuosity and daring

1 Theatre-lovers have acknowledged Laurence Olivier **as one of the greatest actors of the 20th century.**
2 His film performances are recognized **as first-rate,** and his Shakespearean adaptations are considered **(as) unrivalled.**
3 The National Theatre in London appointed him **artistic director.**
4 In 1970, the Queen made Sir Laurence **a life peer.**
5 In the last years of his life he was often chosen **as a character actor.**
6 The critic James Agate considered Olivier **(as) a comedian by instinct and a tragedian by art.**
7 Other critics looked on him **as honest,** but Olivier himself said that he actually regarded acting **as a form of lying.**
8 Other actors might think of their profession **as a form of self-expression,** but Olivier called acting **a way of showing off.**

Note:
The photo shows Lawrence Olivier as King Richard III in the film version of Shakespeare's play.

16 Relative Clauses

Basic Exercises

1 From wealth to poverty

1 a a merchant **who had been so lucky** ... (ll. 1–2): defining
everything **they fancied** (l. 4): defining
... goods **it contained** (l. 8): defining
Their father, **who had ... prospered** ... (ll. 9–10): non-defining
every ship **he had** ... (l. 10): defining
his clerks ..., **whom he trusted entirely** (l. 12): non-defining
All **that he had left** (l. 14): defining
the town **in which he had lived** (l. 15): defining
his children, **who were in despair** ... (l. 16): non-defining
the cottage, **which stood in the midst of a dark forest** (l. 19): non-defining

b a merchant **who/that** ... (ll. 1–2): *who* for persons preferred to *that* in written English
Their father, **who** ... (ll. 9–10): cannot be replaced, as the clause is non-defining
His clerks, **whom/who** ... (l. 12): *whom* is the object case and is preferred in formal English; *that* is not possible here, as the clause is non-defining
All **that/(which)** ... (l. 14): *that* is preferred after the indefinite pronoun *all*
the town **in which** ... (l. 15): cannot be replaced as long as the preposition is placed before the relative pronoun (but cf.: the town **which/that** he had lived **in**)
his children, **who** ... (l. 16): cannot be replaced, as the clause is non-defining
the cottage, **which** ... (l. 19): cannot be replaced, as the clause is non-defining

c Contact clauses in l. 4 *(they fancied)*, l. 8 *(it contained)*, l. 10 *(he had upon the sea)*
The following could be rewritten as contact clauses:
All **that he had left** (l. 13) – All **he had left**
the town **in which he had lived** (l. 15) – the town **he had lived in**

2 ... that he can buy anything **he likes/could wish for,** and his children have every luxury **they fancy/ask for.** But one day his luck is changed by a fire, **which burns his house to the ground/which destroys his house and everything in it.** This is

not the only unfortunate thing **that happens to him/that befalls him and his family.** He also loses the ships **he owns/that belong to him,** and the people **he has always trusted/the people he has employed as clerks/the people who work for him as clerks** are unfaithful to him. So he and his family have to leave the town **they used to live in** and move to a little cottage, **which is in the middle of a dark forest/which is a long way from their old home.** The friends **they used to know/have** are not prepared to help, so there is nothing else **they can do.**

3 a 'Undertakings' are **the things a person does.**
b 'Misfortune' is something unlucky **that happens to someone.**
c 'Precious goods' are things **that are worth a lot of money.**
d 'Pirates' are sailors **who rob other ships (and take them over).**
e 'Wealth' is the money/large sums of money **that a person (or a country, etc.) has.**

4 (free expression of personal experience)

Note on the author:

Born in Scotland, educated at St Andrews and Oxford Universities, **Andrew Lang** (1844–1912) was one of the most prolific writers of his day. Among other things he wrote poetry, essays, reviews, translations and biographies. But today he is best remembered for his collections of fairy-tales, the first of which, his 'Blue Fairy Book', was published in 1889.

2 The cure

... boy, **who was about 17,** ... (l. 2)
... an older man, **who was obviously his father,** ... (l. 3)
... a cow, **which they were about to treat.** (l. 4)
... a red mixture, **which smelled of aniseed,** ... (l. 5)
... Thomas, **who returned the greeting.** (l. 7)
... the hoosh, **which is a disease caused by long worms in a cow's throat.** (l. 8)
... an empty bottle, **which he had put on the shelf beside him.** (l. 10)
... his own medicine, **which was a mixture of linseed oil and turpentine.** (l. 12)
... the things **(which/that) Thomas needed for his mixture** ... (l. 12) (*Note:* This is the only case of a defining relative clause in the text.)

... a teaspoon, **with which Thomas poured the mixture into the cow's nose.** (l. 14)
Thomas, **who had no idea what the effect would be,** ... (l. 14)
The two men, **who were very pleased with the cow's strong reaction,** ... (l. 15)
... the value of the animal, **which he thought was about twenty pounds.** (l. 17)
... the two men, **who were looking at him as if he were a magician.** (l. 20)

3 The body in the library

1 It's the room **the body is found in/where the body is found.**
2 It's the dress **the dead girl has on.**
3 It's the thing **she was killed with.**
4 It's the time **she was murdered at/when she was murdered.**
5 It's the village **Miss Marple comes from/where Miss Marple lives.**
6 He's the man **whose house the police go to first.**
7 She's the person **Basil Blake was seen with the weekend before.**
8 She's the girl **he lives/is living with.**
9 It's the hotel **the dead girl worked at/where the dead girl worked.**
10 She's the girl **Ruby worked with/the girl the police talk to.**
11 It's the time **Ruby danced at/when Ruby danced.**
12 He's the young man **Ruby was last seen (dancing) with.**

4 A puzzle

1 Perhaps people who **don't** get the answer quickly are more sexist in their attitudes than people who **do!**
2 doctor/judge/dentist/architect/electrician/(etc.)

Advanced Exercises

1 Records

1 d ... radio programme, during which Handel's Largo was played, ...
2 f ... televisions, the cost of which was 27 pounds each, ...
3 b ... nine minutes, each of which earned him 2 million dollars.
4 i ... film ever made (...), the first complete performance of which was in Chicago in 1987, ...

16 Relative Clauses

5 a ... child, the TV-watching time of whom is 32 hours a week, ...
6 e ... *White Christmas,* the North American sales of which reached 170 million copies between 1942 and 1987.
7 g ... 28 countries, which is more (countries) than for any other LP.
8 h ... since 1952, which is longer than any other theatre production.
9 c ... railway station, which was because King Edward VII couldn't get into his uniform quickly enough before leaving the train.

2 Relative clauses: formal and informal style

1 **Britain before the Romans:**
... the waters of **what we now call the English Channel and the North Sea** ... (ll. 1–2)
... a few hundreds, **who lived by hunting with the rudely fashioned tools** ... (ll. 5–6)
... tools **they had laboriously chipped from the softer stones about them.** (ll. 6–7)
... a revolution ... in the Near East **which was to change for ever the life of man.** (ll. 9–11)
... the animals **who provided it** ... (l. 13)
... the grasses **he found he could eat** ... (ll. 14–15)
... the food **he desired.** (l. 16)

... the area **they settled on** ... (ll. 23–24)
... men **to whom the sea was a natural barrier.** (ll. 25–26)
... others **for whom it held fewer terrors** ... (ll. 29–30)
... burial places, **whose roof is a great stone.** (l. 34)
... a movement **at whose causes we can only guess,** ... (l. 37)
... a people **who are the first to have left this island ... remains.** (ll. 38–40)
... a language **of which the native tongues ... are the direct descendants.** (ll. 41–43)

A much married man:
... men **who don't like being married.** (l. 1)
... the little things **that women like** and **that some men can't be bothered with.** (ll. 3–4)
... it's attention **a woman wants.** (l. 5)
... it was her money **you were spending.** (l. 11)
It's not the money **that you've paid ... that signifies** ... (ll. 13–14)
... it's the spirit **you give it in.** (ll. 14–15)
That's **what counts with women.** (l. 15)

In the second text, there are a number of clauses introduced by *that* rather than *which* or *who*. There are also three contact clauses (typical of spoken English). There are no non-defining clauses in the text.

2 | **Typical of formal style:** | **Informal alternative:** |
... men ***to whom*** **the sea was a natural barrier.** | ... men ***that*** **saw the sea as a natural barrier.**
... others ***for whom*** **it held fewer terrors.** | ... others ***that*** **were not so afraid of it.**
... burial places, ***whose*** **roof is a great stone.** | ... burial places, ***which*** **have a very large stone as a roof/for a roof.**
... a movement ***at whose*** **causes we can only guess.** | ... a movement **we can only guess the causes *of*.**
... a language ***of which*** **the native tongues ... are the direct descendants.** | ... a language ***that*** **the native tongues of ... are the direct descendants *of*.**

(Four of these are defining relative clauses with the preposition placed before the relative pronoun. The fifth is non-defining, with the genitive *whose*.)

3 a the sea/waters between Britain and Europe, which was/were still widening/still getting wider/getting wider and wider
  b space in which they could live/space they could live in
  c men that lived along the coasts of Spain and Britanny
4 a ... joined the waters of the English Channel, which made Britain an island/which meant that Britain was now an island.
  b ... had a certain fear of the sea, which is understandable/which is hardly surprising.
  c ... considers himself a good husband, which is quite absurd/which is hard to take seriously.
5 ... while the wife was the one **who looked after the home and family.**
Most men wanted a wife **who stayed at home, cooked their meals for them, and waited for them to come home in the evenings after work.**
Women **that had jobs/that wanted to go out to work after they got married/that were financially independent** were unusual.
Women were expected to do **whatever their husbands thought best/decided/told them.**

Housework was a job **that men normally didn't dream of doing/didn't have to do.** (etc.)

Note on the author:

William Somerset Maugham (1874–1965) was born in Paris, but educated in England and later at Heidelberg University. He then trained as a doctor at a London hospital. Soon he became successful as a writer – of plays, novels and short stories. 'Of Human Bondage' (1915), his best-known novel, is largely autobiographical. Although extremely popular as a writer, Maugham sensed that he did not quite belong to the top rank of literary figures, sadly describing himself as 'in the very first row of the second-raters'.

3 Television: Can it be as bad as they say?

One of the few things **most people agree about/ agree on** is that young people watch too much TV/ television/watch TV too much. But **what many people overlook** is the fact that a lot can be learnt/one/you can learn a lot from certain programmes **that are shown on TV.** Crime, violence and soap operas are not the only things **that young people watch.**
But especially/particularly for older/elderly people, **many of whom live alone and so feel lonely/ feel lonely because of this,** television has its advantages/good points/good sides. They see/ look at the families **that appear on TV** almost as their own families – or as real living people, **whose qualities/characteristics they can dicuss/talk about with their friends.** The television set can also represent a kind of friend **that can always be relied on/depended on** – which is particularly important for people who live on their own.
Whatever disadvantages and dangers television may have, we have to realize that it is a part of daily life/our daily lives – just like the telephone or washing machine. We can decide (for) ourselves what role it plays/is to play for us personally.

17 The Use of Adjectives and Adverbs

Basic Exercises

1 Americans and their automobiles

1 naturally (l. 2): d
(not) only (l. 3): a
(but) also (l. 4): a
inevitably (l. 5): a
firmly (l. 7): a
daily (l. 9): a
noticeably (l. 12): a
increasingly (l. 13): b
usually (l. 14): a
densely (l. 16): b
absurdly (l. 17): b
recently (l. 19): a
extremely (l. 19): b
temporarily (l. 23): a
quite (l. 23): c
surprisingly (l. 23): d
fairly (l. 24): b
unexpectedly (l. 24/25): b
terribly (l. 26): c
slowly (l. 26): a
actually (l. 27): d
absolutely (l. 28): b
clearly (l. 31): a
possibly (l. 31): modifies the adverbial phrase *in the not very distant future*
socially (l. 33): b
economically (l. 33): b

2 (is) rooted (l. 7): verb expressing a state = a (can also be seen as a passive form)
(become) common (l. 13): verb expressing a changing state = b
(look) small (l. 17): verb expressing the way something appears to the senses = c
(felt) critical (l. 20): a
(was) easy (l. 24): a
(was) enjoyable (l. 25): a
(are) inaccessible (l. 29): a
(becomes) obsolete (l. 33): b
(are not) sure (l. 34): a

3 a chaotic – I don't like driving into the town centre at this time of day, the traffic is so **chaotic!**

17 The Use of Adjectives and Adverbs

b economic *(wirtschaftlich, Wirtschafts-)* / economical *(sparsam)*
 – If cars were no longer produced in such great numbers, there would be **economic** problems.
 – Our new car ist very **economical** – it uses much less petrol than the old one.

c symbolic(al) – To many Americans, the automobile is **symbolic** of freedom and democracy.

d free – If you go by car, you are **free** to leave when you like and take whichever route you prefer.

e future *(zukünftig)* / futuristic *(futuristisch)*
 – **Future** generations will probably depend more on public transport.
 – Some of the new models displayed at the motor show look very **futuristic**.

4 extremely, quite, surprisingly, fairly, unexpectedly, terribly, actually, absolutely, clearly, socially and economically

The original version of the text contains a number of adverbs that do not add very much new information, but they add emphasis (e.g. *extremely, quite, terribly, clearly*) or express a personal view or comment (e.g. *surprisingly, unexpectedly, actually*) and make the text sound more fluent. The adverbs *socially and economically* could also be left out, but they add interesting extra information. All in all, the text without the 'extra' adverbs sounds more neutral, less persuasive.

5 a These days traffic jams are nothing **unusual**.
 b Drivers who get caught in them can start to feel **aggressive/impatient/angry**.
 c Lots of Americans drive their cars to work **regularly/daily**.
 d The freeways, highways, drive-ins and parking lots in the US have changed the countryside **enormously/noticeably/considerably**.
 e One day cars may become **obsolete**, but right now this doesn't seem **likely/probable**.

1 The dragon

1 Kay found Bob's talk about his relatives **extremely boring**, but she was too **polite** to say so. She **really** didn't want to go to the movies with him, so she **quickly** thought of an excuse, which was so **feeble/unconvincing** that Bob **quickly/immediately/easily** saw through it. Bob told her he felt **worried** about his future, but Kay didn't want to take this remark **seriously**, because she was **afraid** of showing him what she **really** thought of him – that he was **stupid/boring**, and that his future **certainly/probably** wouldn't be **easy/brilliant**. Again, Bob **quickly/immediately** realized what she was **really/actually** thinking, and he **suddenly** decided to tell her the **real/whole** truth. It was the first time Bob and Kay had **really** been **honest** with each other, and as Kay discovered to her **intense/great/enormous** surprise, the truth hurt.

2 She feels a) seasick (cf. l. 3); b) bored (l. 10); c) guilty (l. 42); d) wounded (l. 54); e) angry (ll. 57–59); f) unhappy/depressed/hurt (ll. 70–77).

3 Kay is rather **conceited/self-satisfied**, because she thinks she is superior. She is **smart/clever/intelligent/gifted**, but this makes her rather **unkind/unfair/nasty** towards Bob. She is **dishonest/phony**.
Bob ist **not so smart/clever/gifted**, but he is quick to sense Kay's feelings. Maybe he's a bit **boring**, but at least he's **honest**. He also seems to be **gentle and kind**.
Kay reacts a) **dishonestly/strangely**; b) **angrily/impatiently**.

3 The status-climber

1 He tries to impress people by buying expensive things. If he can afford a small car, he buys a medium-sized one, for example, or if he can afford a large car, he buys another one as an 'extra', even if he doesn't really need a second one. He never buys fakes, but concentrates on things that are obviously expensive.

2 a ... to look just like **real ones**.
 b ... two cars – **a big one** and **a small one**.
 c ... can't afford **an expensive one**.
 d ... but I like **the brown ones**.
 e ... I can recommend **a very good one/a very exciting one**.
 f ... do you prefer – **the blue ones** or **the black ones**?

Note on the author:

Desmond Morris (born in 1928) is the author of a number of very popular books about the behaviour of humans and animals. Among his most successful studies are 'The Naked Ape' (1967) and 'The Human Zoo' (1969), as well as the more recent 'Animalwatching' and 'Manwatching' (1977). He has also made a number of TV series.

Advanced Exercises

1 Chain of violence?

1 ... a very **young one** ...
2 The **terrible thing** ...
3 ... the **sensible thing** would be to insist on a **similar one** ...
4 But the **surprising thing** ... as **small children**, ...
5 ... the **same ones** ...
6 Even **intelligent people** ...
7 The **educated** ... as **simple people** ...
8 The **important thing** ... to protect **the young** ... to treat them as **proper people / human beings** ...
9 ... stating the **obvious**; ... to expect the **impossible**.

2 Similar adverbs – different meanings

1 ... I **hardly** recognized you!
2 I haven't had much time **lately** – I've been working so **hard**.
3 You did **pretty/fairly** well in that quiz – you got most of the answers **right**.
4 ... – Quite **rightly** in my opinion. After all, he really wasn't playing **fair**.
5 It's still **fairly/pretty** early – but that's good. We don't want to risk arriving **late**.
6 ... You've arranged them so **prettily**.

18 Adjectives and Adverbs: Comparative and Superlative Forms

Basic Exercises

1 Some good, some bad, all different

1 one of the **biggest** collections (l. 1): superlative formed from an adjective of one syllable
the **most valuable** thing (l. 4): superlative form (adjective of three syllables)
the **best** of them (l. 10 + l. 11): irregular superlative form of *good*
They are **better** people (l. 11): irregular comparative form of *good*
They are **cleaner** people (l. 12): comparative formed from an adjective of one syllable
They are **kinder-hearted** people (l. 12): comparative formed from an adjective of one syllable, here used as a compound
Most men (l. 16): irregular superlative form of *many*
I **don't** get to meet **as many women as** I'd like to (l. 17): comparison with *not as ... as*.
My ... work does **not** bring me into contact with them **as much as** I would wish (l. 18–19): comparison with *not as ... as*

2 He 'collects' people because he thinks they are the most valuable – or interesting – 'thing' there is. He finds them interesting because they are all so different. He likes women best because he finds them superior people; he finds them kinder, better and cleaner than men. He also feels he can talk to women better / more easily than to men, because they are better listeners.

3 Perhaps his father did**n't** have **as much** time for him **as** his mother. His teachers (at kindergarten / at school) may have had a great influence on him; perhaps the women that taught him were **kinder/ gentler** than the men.
It's possible that he always made friends with girls **more easily than** with boys. Perhaps he has seen a lot of films about violent men and unfairly treated women. (etc.)

4 (free expression of personal opinion)

Note on the author:

Alan Ayckbourn was born into an artistic family in 1939; his father was a musician and his mother a writer. He went into acting as soon as he left school, aged 17. His first plays were written to earn a little money, as he was not paid well as an actor, but he soon discovered that his greatest talent was for writing rather than acting. He runs his own theatre in Scarborough, on the Yorkshire coast, for which all his plays were originally written. Now he is one of Britain's most successful and popular playwrights; his plays are comedies of suburban and middle-class life. 'A Talk in the Park' is one of a collection of plays entitled 'Confusions', which were produced in the Apollo theatre in London in 1976 (cf. the students' edition of 'Confusions', Klett-Nr. 5795)

2 Human aggression

1 aggressive – hardly – certain – habitually – positive – generally – most repulsive – brutal – bestial – characteristic – less highly developed – brutal – savage – sombre – cruellest – most ruthless

The adjectives **'brutal'** and **'bestial'** are **generally** supposed to describe behaviour that is **characteristic** of animals, but in fact the **less highly developed** creatures of this earth do not show such **aggressive/savage** behaviour towards each other as we do. Man is the **cruellest** and **most ruthless** creature in the world. This can **hardly** be doubted.

2 least repulsive (or: most beautiful/most attractive); more highly developed; least cruel (or: kindest/gentlest/most loving)

3 Man is certainly **more aggressive than** most animals.
A lot of people like dogs **better than** cats, because they seem to be **more loving/more dependent** on their owners.
Nowadays cattle are much **more useful than** horses because of the food they provide.
Some people find wild animals **more interesting** than pets, because they can be studied/watched/observed in their natural environment.
Robots can do certain jobs **more efficiently than** people.
Modern weapons are a much **greater** threat/danger to mankind **than** primitive weapons ever were. (etc.)

Note on the author:

Born in 1920, **Anthony Storr** studied medicine at Cambridge University, and later specialized in psychiatry. As well as numerous newspaper articles and reviews, he has written a number of books on human behaviour. 'Human Aggression', dedicated to Konrad Lorenz, was published in 1968.

Advanced Exercises

1 Buy, buy, buy

1 a to get **more** – and **better** – things
b it makes poor people want **more and more** things/luxuries
c the poor have **more** money and comfort **than** they ever had before
d some days are **less exciting than** others; there are always **more** days of work **than** there are days of excitement and sports
e it makes people feel that they haven't got **as much as** they want (to have), and makes them unhappy because of this

2 Advertising works more effectively on the poor because they have no way of knowing that true happiness cannot be bought with materials goods. Rich people are more likely to realize this.

3 Perhaps the author means that if he spends so much time working, he will never have enough time to learn how to surf properly; his physical condition will probably not be good enough.

4 In many ways people probably **did** feel happier in the days before television and mass advertising. Ordinary people have now come to expect all sorts of luxuries that would have been unthinkable years ago. Holidays abroad are just one example of the sort of thing that used to be considered a luxury but is now nothing unusual.
Years ago, when it was still unusual for married women to earn money of their own, families used to spend more time together at home, and life was less hectic.
Most people had a lower standard of living, but in many ways their actual quality of life was probably much better.

5 (free expression of personal experience)

6 a The harder you work, **the less time you have for other activities.**
b The more material possessions you have, **the more you want to get.**
c The better educated a person is, **the better chance they should have of a good job.**
d The more you know about the tricks used in advertising, **the less easily you feel persuaded to buy the products.**

Note on the author:

Charles A. Reich was born in New York in 1928 and became a teacher of law at Yale University. 'The Greening of America', which appeared in 1970 and was praised as an 'extraordinary' and 'enormously interesting' book, quickly became a classic best-seller.

2 Were people more aggressive then?

... we tend to think that people living in **earlier** centuries were **more aggressive/more brutal** than people today. ... there were no law courts, and people were often **cruelly/severely/unjustly** punished by the Sheriff, even for **small/trivial** crimes like stealing firewood ... In those **medieval/faraway/primitive** days, a person could be put to death for committing a crime no **more serious/worse/more terrible** than stealing a loaf of bread. In the 17th century, ..., the streets of London were much **more dangerous** than they are today, and people behaved altogether **more violently/more savagely/more riotously** than they **usually/normally** do now. The **worst/most violent** of all the Londoners were the watermen, ... They were so **violent** that they prevented the building of bridges over the Thames, as they feared this would mean **fewer** passengers for them – and **less** money. The 17th century was probably one of the **cruellest/most violent/most bloodthirsty** times in history; **enormous/vast/huge** crowds came to watch the **brutal** public executions, and it is **hard/difficult** to imagine a **more terrible/more repulsive** sight than the heads of the executed prisoners ...

Travelling was **more difficult/slower** and **more dangerous/riskier** than it is today, because of the **terrible/bad** condition of the roads, and because of highwaymen. By the 18th century, however, roads had become far **better,** so coaches were able to travel **faster/more quickly,** making it **harder/more difficult** for robbers to attack. But there were still a few highwaymen, the **most famous/most dangerous/worst** of them being Dick Turpin, who was **finally/eventually** caught and hanged in 1739. Today, of course, the legal system works **better/more efficiently** than in those days, there is a **properly/well** organized police force, and punishments are **more humane/less severe.** But it is **doubtful** whether people **really/actually** behave less aggressively/better towards each other than they used to.

3 Advertising techniques

1 New 'scientific discoveries' are used in adverts in order to **make the product seem more effective.**
2 With the help of photographic tricks, products can **be made to look more attractive than they really are.**
3 The advertiser repeats the name of the product again and again so that **people will remember it more easily.**
4 If the product is recommended by 'experts' such as well-known personalities, **people probably feel they can rely on it more/feel it is safer to use.**
5 Suggesting that all the 'best' people use a certain product is supposed to make us worry that if we don't use it, **we somehow won't be as successful/attractive/... as other people.**

19 The Position of Adverbs and Adverbials

Basic Exercises

1 Going to college

1 **After high school** a lot of American students choose to do a ... college or university program./A lot of American students choose to do a ... program **after high school.**
2 A university is **usually** different from a college in that it is much bigger./A university is different ... in that it is **usually** much bigger.
3 But **generally** the word 'college' is used to describe both./But the word 'college' is **generally** used ...
4 **Normally** a university has an undergraduate college .../A university **normally** has ...
5 **Nowadays** you have to be in the top half of your high school class to have a chance of getting into a college or university./You have to be ... or university **nowadays.**
6 The 'Ivy League' colleges ... are **extremely** famous.
7 **Not surprisingly,** it is difficult to get a place at one of these.

19 The Position of Adverbs and Adverbials

8. **Now** most of them are co-educational. / Most of them are **now** co-educational. / ... are co-educational **now**.
9. But they are **traditionally** linked with female colleges ...
10. The guidance counsellor (...) is **specially** trained to advise students ...
11. As there are so many different kinds of college, each student must consider the alternatives **carefully**.
12. That is **always** important.
13. For a serious-minded person, a college specializing in academics would **certainly** be the right choice.
14. But for someone athletic, a college emphasizing sports **probably** offers more.
15. **During the summer vacation** most students work to help finance their studies. / Most students work **during the summer vacation** to help finance their studies. / ... work to help finance their studies **during the summer vacation**.
16. Some **even** have regular part-time jobs.
17. Getting into college isn't **terribly** difficult.
18. But **unfortunately** quite a number of people flunk out before they finish their studies.

2 Homeless in London

Keith: My home is a cardboard box **in a car park near the Royal Festival Hall.** I've been unemployed **for four years.**
I came **to London** to look for work. But **I soon** discovered / But **soon** I discovered London isn't the Utopia it's **so often** made out to be.

Barry: The big trouble **in London** is finding a place to live. Landlords **nearly always** demand two months' rent **in advance.**
But if you're **only** making two or three pounds **an hour** doing casual work **in a restaurant**, it's **almost** impossible to get that much money together **at one time.**

Steve: A tea van **usually** comes round **at eleven o'clock at night.** Or if you have 20p, you can get a cup of coffee **at the kiosk outside Waterloo Station.**
And if you have 10p left, you can **even** enjoy the warmth of the station's indoor toilets **for a few minutes.** But you can't stay **there very long.** The police check the place **regularly.**

Bruce: I look for work **every day.** But it's difficult if you aren't dressed **in clean clothes at the interview.**
People **just** treat you **differently** when you look scruffy. They **sometimes even** pretend they haven't seen you. / They **sometimes** pretend they haven't **even** seen you.

Keith: There's a strong code of ethics **in the homeless community.** A newcomer made a mistake **here a few days ago.** He took someone else's piece of cardboard to protect himself **from the wind.**
He was **politely** told to put it back **immediately**, and someone said **jokingly:** 'Stealing someone's bed **already**?'

Bruce: **Sometimes** I **really** don't mind / I **sometimes really** don't mind feeling hungry, / I **really** don't mind feeling hungry **sometimes,** because I know there are other people who are hungry, too. **Strangely enough,** whenever I get some money, I **always** end up giving it away to someone who needs it **more.**

Advanced Exercises

1 The disastrous growth of world population

World population / The population of the world is now increasing more quickly than ever before, and in the next hundred years it might even triple / and it might even triple in the next hundred years. But this would have disastrous consequences, especially for the environment.
According to a United Nations report, which was published in London yesterday, the population of the Earth will grow by 90 to 100 million people a year in the next decade. Unfortunately population grows fastest / most quickly in the poorest developing countries. The best and quickest way to slow down / of slowing down population growth / the growth of population is probably to improve the status of women in these countries and to offer them the chance of a proper training in future. Naturally / Of course it is especially / particularly important to invest in family planning in the developing countries. Yearly expenditure for this will possibly have to be doubled by the end of this century.

2 Some positive effects of immigration

1. **Only rarely do** people **stop** to consider ... (ll. 3–4): People **only rarely stop** to consider ...
   no sooner had the factory gates **opened** ... than the traditional ... closed his doors. (ll. 7–9): The factory gates **had no sooner opened** in the evening than the traditional ... closed his doors.
   Not only have Asian people **improved** the trades ... (l. 11): Asian people **have not only improved** the trades ...

Never before has such a wide range ... **been** available in Britain. (ll. 16–18): Such a wide range ... **has never been** available in Britain before.
So great have been the problems of assimilation in some areas that ... (ll. 19–20): The problems of assimilation **have been so great** in some areas that ...
Not for all the world should the problems ... **be allowed** to let us forget ... (ll. 23–25): The problems some immigrants have created **should not for all the world be allowed** to let us forget ...

2 Nur selten macht man sich die Mühe, an die positiven Veränderungen, die die Einwanderer mit herbeigeführt haben, zu denken. Damals in den fünfziger Jahren konnten Arbeiter während der Woche nicht zum Einkaufen gehen: Kaum hatten sich die Fabriktore am Abend geöffnet, da schloß der traditionelle britische Ladenbesitzer seine Türen.
Die Asiaten haben nicht nur das Bild der Berufe, die sie ergriffen haben, verbessert, ihre harte Arbeit / ihr Fleiß gibt den Briten darüber hinaus ein Beispiel / dient ... als Beispiel.
Nie zuvor gab es in Großbritannien eine so reiche Auswahl an köstlichen Speisen / Nahrungsmitteln.
Die Probleme der Integration (der Einwanderer) waren (und sind) in manchen Gegenden so groß, daß die Briten geneigt sind, die überlegenen Eigenschaften vieler asiatischer Familien zu übersehen, deren Zusammengehörigkeitsgefühl und Verantwortungsbewußtsein unsere von Ehescheidungen zerrüttete Gesellschaft in einem sehr schwachen Licht erscheinen lassen. Nicht um alles in der Welt dürfen uns die Probleme, für die einige Einwanderer verantwortlich sind, dazu bringen, den guten Einfluß zu vergessen, den andere ausgeübt haben.

3 Different styles

1 The text by P. D. James contains a fairly large number of adjectives and adverbs, most of them used to give extra 'colour' to the narrative.

Examples of adjectives that have such a function: sharp (l. 7); absolute (l. 11).

Examples of adverbs that have such a function: dreadfully (l. 3); instinctively (l. 3); immediately (l. 6); instantly (l. 10); instinctively (l. 14); tightly (l. 18); brightly (l. 19).

The text by Ernest Hemingway contains a number of adjectives, but they are strictly 'necessary' to the narrative, rather than serving a 'decorative' function.

Examples:
dark (l. 6); black (l. 12); tight (l. 14); same (l. 16); different (l. 17); tight (l. 18).
The Hemingway text contains no adverbs (apart from the adverb of place *outside* in line 6).

2 P. D. James uses a very descriptive, atmospheric style. Her vivid use of adjectives and adverbs help to create a mysterious atmosphere in this passage from 'A Taste for Death'. A special effect is created by the way she 'interrupts' sentences with the addition of descriptive adverbs and adverbials (e.g. l. 1: And it was then, **in that moment,** that she felt ...; ll. 5–6: And then, **immediately,** he was back at her side.). The style is not particularly complex, but it has a personal, emotional quality.
Hemingway's style is straightforward and concise. He uses simple descriptions of people and scenes. The narrative is presented in an unemotional way, and no unnecessary 'extras' are added.
(+ free expression of personal opinion)

3 The door of Henry's lunch-room **suddenly** opened and two men came in. They sat down **quietly** at the counter.
'What's yours?' George asked them **in a friendly voice.**
'I don't know,' one of the men said **sullenly.** 'I really don't know what I want to eat.'
Outside **in the street** it was **slowly** getting dark.
A few minutes later the street light came on outside the window. The two men at the counter read the menu **carefully.** From the other end of the counter Nick Adams watched them **curiously.** He had been talking to George about the menu when they came in.

These changes make the text much less impressive, because the additions are unnecessary, and spoil the simplicity of the style. The 'typical' atmosphere of this Hemingway extract immediately disappears, and the style becomes duller.

Note on the authors:

One of Britain's most popular detective novelists, **Phyllis Dorothy James** (born 1920) worked for nearly twenty years an as administrator for the National Health Service. In 1968 she began working for the Police Department of the Home Office, and joined the children's division of the Criminal Department in 1971. Her experiences in these various fields gave her valuable material for her books. 'A Taste for Death' was first published in 1986.

Ernest Hemingway (1899–1961) is recognized as a master of the art of short story writing. He was born in Illinois, the son of a doctor. After working in Kansas City as a reporter, he served as a volunteer on the Italian front in 1918. Later he settled in Paris.

His first stories, poems and novels were published in the 1920s. His collection 'Men Without Women', which includes 'The Killers', appeared in 1927. He gave active support to the Republicans during the Spanish Civil War, and was a war correspondent in Europe during the Second World War. Apart from his short stories, Hemingway's most successful works are probably 'The Sun Also Rises' (1926), 'A Farewell to Arms' (1929), set on the Italian front in the First World War, 'For Whom the Bell Tolls' (1940) with its background of the Spanish Civil War, and his masterpiece in novella form, 'The Old Man and the Sea' (1952), about the struggle of man against nature. He was awarded the Nobel Prize for Literature in 1954. After a long and serious illness, Hemingway shot himself in 1961.

20 The Definite and the Indefinite Article

Basic Exercises

1 Life-saving

1 a She was **an American.** (or: She was **American** – 'American' is an adjective here.)
 b They should learn it at **school.**
 c He is **an anaesthetist.**
 d They mostly drown because **the temperature** of their body drops in **very cold water.**
 e First **the memory** stops working and then **the person** becomes unconscious. This is **hypothermia.**
 f You should do this 15 or 16 times **a minute.**
 g It should be massaged once **a second.**
 h It is called this because by 'kissing' the unconscious person and breathing air into **the mouth,** you can bring **the person** back to **life.**

2 **a** now healthy ... five-year-old (ll. 1–2)
 pulled from **the** freezing waters of **the** Great Salt Lake (ll. 2–3)
 She had been in **the** water for over **an** hour. (ll. 3–4)
 If **the** girl had been **a** Briton ... (l. 6) – The indefinite article would be left out in German.
 The problem is ... (l. 7)
 what to do in **an** emergency (l. 11)
 the temperature of their body drops (ll. 13–14)
 Tony Simcock, **an** anaesthetist ... (ll. 14–15) – The indefinite article could be left out in German.
 at **the** Royal Cornwall Hospital ... (l. 15)
 the real reason ... (ll. 16–17)
 When **the** temperature of **the** body drops ..., **the** memory stops ... (ll. 17–19)
 as **the** head slips into **the** water (ll. 20–21)
 The average time **a** victim can survive in water at 5 degrees is **an** hour (ll. 21–22)
 such **an** emergency (l. 23) – In German the indefinite article could be placed before or after *solch*.
 call **an** expert – maybe **a** doctor (l. 24)
 clear **the** victim's airway (l. 25)
 put **the** body flat on **the** ground, with **the** head lower than **the** rest (ll. 25–26)
 cover **the** victim's nose, and breathe into **the** mouth ... (l. 27)
 15 or 16 times **a** minute (l. 28) – In German *in* + the definite article would be used.
 Massage **the** heart once **a** second. (ll. 28–29) – Instead of the indefinite article, *in* + the definite article would be used in German.
 Keep **the** victim warm, ... (l. 29)
 until **the** expert arrives (l. 30)

3 Vor drei Jahren wurde ein jetzt (völlig) gesundes fünfjähriges amerikanisches Mädchen aus dem eiskalten Wasser des Großen Salzsees gezogen. Sie schien tot zu sein. Sie war über eine Stunde lang im Wasser gewesen. Nachdem zwei Stunden lang erste Hilfe geleistet wurde, wurde sie **ins Leben** zurückgerufen.
Wenn das Mädchen Britin gewesen wäre, wäre sie wahrscheinlich gestorben. Das Problem ist, daß **die Kenntnisse** in elementarer erster Hilfe / **die Grundkenntnisse** in erster Hilfe in Großbritannien sehr begrenzt sind. Hilfe muß schnell geleistet werden – und beharrlich. **Die meisten Kinder** erhalten **in der Schule** keine richtige Ausbildung (in erster Hilfe) und wissen nicht, was sie in einem Notfall tun sollen.

Die meisten Menschen, die ertrinken, tun dies, weil sie **im eiskalten Wasser** in Schwierigkeiten geraten und ihre Körpertemperatur sinkt.

Further differences between German and English: In German the definite article is used in a number of cases where there is no article in English; cf. the noun phrases in **bold type**.

2 An English secret

Tea is best made in **a brown china teapot**. First you warm **the pot** with **hot water**, which you throw away after **a moment** or two. Then put in **a teaspoonful** of **tea** for each person, and **an extra one** for luck ('one for **the pot**'). Now pour **boiling water** on, and leave **the tea** to stand for three to five minutes, before pouring it into **fine china cups**, with or without **milk** and **sugar**. **Hot water** is served separately, to make **the tea** less strong. Philip Sidley is **a tea expert**. He believes that **the secret** of good tea lies in **the quality** of **the water** you use. Jonathan Goodall, who is the manager of **a big firm** of **tea importers**, does not think **the type** of **water** is **such an important aspect**. He says **the main thing** is to make **the tea** immediately after **the water** has boiled.
Queen Elizabeth the Second would agree with Philip Sidley. Whenever she travels away from **home**, she takes **a special type** of **English spring water** with her – for making **tea**.
Although **coffee** is also drunk a lot in England today, **the drinking** of **tea** is closely connected with **a certain philosophy** of **life**. Tea-drinking is regarded as **a ceremony**, not just as **a way** of quenching one's thirst. **People** drink **tea** to forget – if only for **half an hour** or so – **the worries** of **daily life**.

Advanced Exercises

1 Questions about the universe

1 a **thought** (l. 3): abstract noun – used here with *little;* but even if *thought* stood alone, it would have no article, as it is not defined / it is used in a general sense
the machinery (l. 3): uncountable singular noun – with an article because it is defined by a relative clause
the sunlight (l. 4): uncountable singular noun – with an article because it is defined by a relative clause
life (l. 4): abstract noun – no article because it is used in a general sense / it is not defined
the gravity (l. 5): abstract noun – with an article because it is defined by a relative clause
space (l. 6): abstract noun – without an article because it is used in a general sense / it is not defined
stability (l. 7): abstract noun – used here with *whose;* the article would be used, however, if the phrase were: '... on **the stability** of which ...
time (l. 10): abstract noun – used here with *much;* but even if *time* stood alone, it would have no article, as it is not defined
nature (l. 11): abstract noun – without an article, as it is used in a general sense
matter (l. 18): uncountable singular noun – without an article, as it is used in a general sense
the past; the future (l. 19): these abstract nouns are always used with the article, except in the phrase 'in future'
chaos; order (ll. 20/21): abstract nouns – without articles because they are used in a general sense
human understanding (l. 27): abstract noun – preceded by an adjective, but used in a general sense, so no article is needed
philosophy and science (l. 28): abstract nouns – without articles because they are used in a general sense
b **Expensive machinery / Complex machinery** is needed in most factories and industries.
There would be no life on Earth without **sunlight**. / People often wear dark glasses in **bright sunlight**.
Gravity is the force that keeps us on the Earth.

2 Wir machen uns kaum Gedanken über den Mechanismus, der das Sonnenlicht erzeugt, das **das Leben** ermöglicht, über die Schwerkraft, die uns an eine Erde klebt, die uns sonst in **den Weltraum** hinausschleudern würde, oder über die Atome, aus denen wir bestehen und von deren Stabilität wir grundsätzlich abhängen. Außer **(den) Kindern** / Von **(den) Kindern** abgesehen (die noch nicht genug wissen, um nicht die wichtigen Fragen zu stellen), verschwenden / verbringen nur wenige von uns viel Zeit damit, sich zu fragen, warum **die Natur** so ist wie sie ist; woher der Kosmos stammt oder ob es ihn (schon) immer gegeben hat; ob **die Zeit** eines Tages rückwärts laufen wird und **die Wirkungen den Ursachen** vorausgehen werden; oder ob es endgültige Grenzen für menschliches Wissen gibt.

3 a Without **the warmth/the heat/the light** that is given off by the sun, **life** on our Earth would be impossible.
   b Because of **the force/the power/the law** of **gravity**, a ball you throw up into **the air** will inevitably come down again.
   c **Chaos** is a state in which nothing is ordered; but when we observe **nature** on our planet – **the life** and **(the) development/(the) growth** of animals and plants, for example – we find ...
   d According to **the theory** of relativity, it is impossible for any normal object to travel faster than **the speed** of **light**.

Note on the authors:

Carl Sagan (born in New York in 1934), Professor of Astronomy and Space Sciences and Director of the Laboratory of Planetary Studies at Cornell University in Ithaca, specializes in the search for extraterrestrial life and intelligence. As a scientific adviser of NASA, he worked on the Viking and Voyager space probe programmes. Among his numerous publications are 'Cosmos' (1980), which was also turned into a very successful TV series, and 'The Dragons of Eden', which was awarded the Pulitzer Prize in 1978.

Stephen Hawking (born in 1944) is Professor of Mathematics at Cambridge University. He is widely regarded as the most brilliant theoretical physicist since Einstein. Hawking is severely physically handicapped and has been confined to a wheelchair since the 1960s. In 'A Brief History of Time' (1988), his first book for the non-specialist reader, he explores the questions of the origin of the universe and the nature of time. The book quickly became a non-fiction best-seller.

2 Agatha Christie

Agatha Christie, **the most famous detective story writer** of **all time,** was born in Torquay (Devon) in 1890. She never went to **school,** for her parents had her educated at **home.** As **a young woman** she went to Paris, where she studied music with the intention of becoming **a singer.** In 1914 she got married, and when the First World War broke out, she worked as **a hospital dispenser** in/at a hospital in Torquay. Her accurate/detailed knowledge of poisons, which she later showed in her novels, originated from the time (she spent) at/in this hospital.
During this period/At this time she began to read detective novels; these stories made **such a big impression** on her that she decided to try her own luck as **an author.** 'The Mysterious Affair at Styles', the first of over 60 detective novels, appeared in 1920. 'The Murder of Roger Ackroyd', a novel about murder, suicide and blackmail, was published in 1926 and is recognized as **a masterpiece** of **detective fiction.**
Agatha Christie, the 'Queen of **Crime**', died in 1976. Her books, however, live on, and have already been translated into more than **a hundred** languages. No wonder that the names 'Hercule Poirot' and 'Miss Marple' now mean at least as much for **most people** as 'Sherlock Holmes'.

3 When I'm alone

1 age, loneliness, change (l. 4); life (l. 8): all abstract nouns used generally
   inmost faith (l. 10): abstract noun with an adjective, but used in a general sense
   the stillness (l. 9): abstract noun with an article, because it is defined by 'where our spirits walk'

2 The poem is about being alone/solitude/loneliness.
   Other abstract themes that often appear in poetry: death; love; war; (un)happiness; nature; religion; guilt; jealousy; remorse; time; childhood; youth; music; philosophy; (etc.)

Note on the author:

Best known for his war poetry, with its stark realism, contempt for blind patriotism, and deep feelings for his fellow-soldiers, **Siegfried Sassoon** (1886–1967) even threw away the British military award he was given for his courage in the front line during the First World War. By the 1920s his reputation as a poet was established. He was also fairly successful as a prose writer; most of his books were largely autobiographical.

21 Indefinite Pronouns and Determines

Basic Exercises

1 Famous words

1 The 'many' are all the people who hear the word of God / who learn about Christ's teachings. The 'few' are the few people who actually follow Christ. God calls them – and chooses them.
2 Some **people**; too much **money / wealth / good fortune**; little **money / wealth / luck**
Money and material things do not make people happy. The main things is to appreciate what one has, however little that may be.
3 everyone / everybody
None is used to avoid repeating the noun *faces*.
4 *A little* means 'some' or 'a small quantity' of something. But *little* in Nr. 2 means 'not much at all' or 'hardly any(thing)'.
'A little knowledge' can be dangerous because knowing only part of the truth can lead to mistakes or misunderstandings.
5 *All men* refers to every person on earth; *all the people* refers to all the persons living in a certain country / the USA.
Lincoln may have meant that a politician's mistakes cannot remain hidden for long. The truth always comes out in the end.
6 Animals ... **do not** ask **any** questions, and **do not** pass **any** criticisms.
7 If everyone is given a position of importance, nobody is really important any more.
8 *Anybody* means 'it doesn't matter who'. *Everybody* would be wrong here.
9 **Nothing** is ever done about it.
Jeder redet vom Wetter, aber keiner unternimmt etwas dagegen.
10 **Too much** of what you fancy **doesn't do** you good. / It **is not** good for you to have **too much** of what you like or enjoy.
Note:
This saying is always used in a **positive** sense, however, meaning that it is healthy to do what you enjoy, as long as you don't overdo it.
11 The 'few' were the British people / pilots who fought in the battle (up in the air) to defend their country from the Germans. The 'many' were the ordinary people of Britain who did not take part in the fighting.
12 *Any* is used to mean 'it doesn't matter what / who'.
Wir werden jede Last tragen, jeden Freund unterstützen, jedem Feind Widerstand leisten, um das Überleben und den Erfolg der Freiheit zu gewährleisten / sichern.

2 Born again

... **every** day (l. 1) ... **Nobody** cared about **anything / anybody**. **Nothing** had **any** meaning (l. 2) ... I had **nothing** to do, didn't want to see **anybody**. **Everything** was zero. I was just waiting for **someone** ... (l. 4) ... I didn't have **any** answers. (l. 9) ... I don't know **anything** (l. 10) ... now I can talk to **anyone** – old ladies, kids, **anyone**. (ll. 14–15)

3 Rangers – few spectators and little enthusiasm

2 So far they haven't won **as many** games **as** in previous seasons.
3 **Some** of their players ...
4 The club has **some / several** good players, but so far they haven't scored **many** goals.
5 **Not many** spectators ... / **Hardly any** spectators ...
6 **Not many** towns / **Hardly any** towns ..., but **not many people** want to ... / **hardly anyone** wants to ...
7 The club must have **some** money left ... the management hasn't given **much** thought ...
8 **Not much** has been done ... / **Hardly anything** has been done ...
9 Now there aren't **many** matches left to play.
10 ... **a bit of** patience / **some** patience.

Advanced Exercises

1 The Story-Teller

1 a ... **each** of the three girls ...
b **Few** people ...
c But **all** the girls ...
d ... **all** her three medals.
e **Each** of them ...
f ... **anyone** else ... as **many** as three medals.
g ... **any** children ...
h ... were **both** afraid of sheep.
i **Neither** of them wanted **any** sheep or clocks around.
j ... **no** flowers ... unable to pick **any**.
k Only very **few** people ...

1 ...there was **nothing** left ... **a few/some** bits of clothing, **both** her shoes and **all** the three medals.... **none** of the pigs ...

2 l. 4: *A little girl* means 'a small girl' (*little* is used as an adjective).
Little interest means 'not much interest' (*little* is not an adjective here, but an indefinite determiner).
l. 5: She did **everything** she was told.
l. 10: You are **all** prettier than she was. / **All** of you are prettier ...
l. 15: ... she won **a few/some** medals ...
l. 21: *Many* is used because it refers to *medals,* a countable plural noun. *Much* can only be used with uncountable nouns.
l. 25: **All the people in the neighbourhood/in the country** talked about ...
ll. 34–36/42–48: *No* is more formal, and typical of written style (here: the bachelor is telling his story as a proper narrative, and chooses a more formal style in parts). *Not ... any* is more typical of conversation, and therefore preferred by the little girls asking questions about the story.
l. 56: *not many/few*

Note on the author:

Hector Hugo Munro (1870–1916) used **'Saki'** as his pen-name. He was born in Burma, but brought up in England. He is famous for his short stories, many of which illustrate animals as agents of revenge upon the human race. In 1914 he enlisted as a trooper for service in the First World War, and was killed in France.

2 Life's too short for doing dishes

Everyone knows that life is short. But only very **few** people realize how **much** of this short time we waste. Let's imagine/suppose you spend about 20 minutes washing up after **each** meal. That means that **everyone** that has to wash up stands at the kitchen sink for about an hour **every** day. That makes/is seven hours **every** week/a week, over two weeks **every** year/a year. And so/in this way **some** people waste two years of their life – unless they buy (themselves) a dishwasher/washing-up machine.
Nobody particularly likes washing up/likes washing up much; **anyone** who has ever stood/worked in the kitchen after Christmas dinner/after lunch on Christmas Day, knows that it is**n't much** fun.
We have dishwashers in **all** sizes, to fit **every/any** kitchen. Our machines (can) clean/wash practically **everything,** however dirty/it doesn't matter how dirty your dishes are.

22 Reflexive and Reciprocal Pronouns

Basic Exercises

1 Self-esteem

1 a The assertive woman can accept herself as she is, and allows herself to have faults.
  b The more you value yourself, the easier it is to listen to other people's criticism, and to learn from it instead of finding fault with yourself too much.
  c Changing is a risk, but women can take this risk if they learn to feel open and free to be themselves.

2 Selma akzeptiert sich (selbst) so wie sie *ist,* was bedeutet, daß sie ihre Stärken und Schwächen (an)erkennt. Je mehr sie sich selbst achtet und **sich** ihrer Stärke **bewußt wird/sich** stark **fühlt,** desto mehr kann sie es sich erlauben, diejenigen ihrer Eigenschaften zu sehen/zu betrachten, die sie nicht besonders mag, die sie aber akzeptieren kann. Je mehr sie sich selbst in ihren eigenen Grenzen akzeptiert, um so mehr ist sie bereit, **(sich)** die Kritik anderer (Menschen) **anzuhören** und daraus zu lernen, ohne in Selbstvorwürfe zu versinken. Je offener sie **sich fühlt,** um so freier ist sie, sie selbst zu sein. Sie kann das Risiko eingehen, **sich** zu **ändern,** ohne **sich** verzweifelt an das Bekannte und Vertraute zu **klammern.**

3 a If you are *self-centred,* you are only interested in yourself and your own enjoyment.
  b *Self-control* is the ability to keep yourself/oneself under control/to control your/one's feelings.
  c *Self-defence* is the art of fighting against anyone or anything that attacks you.

d A *self-help book* advises readers how they can help themselves to improve their lives.
e *Self-pity* means feeling sorry for oneself.
f A *self-portrait* is a picture that an artist has painted of himself/herself.
g A *self-service restaurant* is a place where customers help themselves to food and drinks instead of waiting at a table to be served.

Note on the author:

Anne Dickson was born in 1946. She studied psychology, and after a visit to America in 1976, she began teaching assertiveness training in Britain. 'A Woman in Your Own Right' was published in 1982.

2 The tale of Hansel and Gretel

Do you still **remember** the tale/fairy tale/story of Hansel and Gretel? Their parents are poor, and **decide** to take/lead the children into the forest/the woods and leave them there. When the children notice that they are alone, they first try to **comfort each other.** But they **lose their way** in the forest. When they **get/come** to the gingerbread house, they **feel glad/pleased/very happy.** But the door **opens** and an old witch comes out. The witch locks Hansel up in a cage, and Gretel **wonders** how she can **save/rescue herself** and her brother. When Gretel has pushed the witch into the hot oven and has freed Hansel/has set Hansel free, the two children **hug each other.** There is a box full of gold coins in the witch's house. The children **take** the treasure **(for themselves)** and **set off** happily towards home/set off home happily.

Advanced Exercises

1 Ernest and the two girls

1 a They don't notice him at first because they are so engrossed in **themselves**, talking to **each other.**
  b He shakes **himself** free of his negative thoughts about **himself,** and concentrates on the girls and their problems.
  c They whisper to **each other** and watch him go to the counter.
  d The other people in the café are too absorbed in **themselves** to notice anything/anyone else.

2 a) to remember (l. 13); b) to move (l. 18); c) looked at each other (l. 9); d) leaning (l. 20); e) had happened (l. 13); f) wondered (l. 11); g) to stretch (l. 11); h) withdrew into himself (l. 10); i) shook himself free (l. 18).

3 The author's use of the reciprocal pronoun *each other* ('the two girls looked at **each other**', l. 9; 'whispering to **each other**', ll. 32–33; 'they glanced at **each other**', l. 43) shows the closeness of the two sisters and suggests that they belong together and are never alone. Two of the examples of reflexive pronouns refer to Ernest's situation ('he withdrew into **himself**', l. 10; ... shook **himself** free of such thoughts', ll. 18–19) and underline his feelings of loneliness. The other examples ('engrossed in **themselves**', l. 1; 'so absorbed in **themselves**', l. 45) seem to emphasize the fact that Ernest is alone with his problems and nobody else has time to be interested in him or his life.
Note:
'... the atmosphere between **himself** and the two girls' (l. 47) is an example of a reflexive pronoun used as an alternative to the personal pronoun *him*' (cf. GhE 87.1 A).

Note on the author:

Born one of five children in 1928, **Alan Sillitoe** was brought up in Nottingham, the son of an illiterate working-class father. He started work in a bicycle factory at the age of 14, and later served in the Royal Air Force in Malaya. His interest in reading – and writing – developed when he was in hospital for 18 months, recovering from tuberculosis. His first novel, 'Saturday Night and Sunday Morning' (1958), highly praised, is about the life of a young factory worker in Nottingham. He has published a number of other successful novels, and has also written poetry and plays. 'Uncle Ernest' is taken from his 1959 collection of short stories, 'The Loneliness of the Long Distance Runner' (the title story, about a rebellious Borstal boy, is one of Sillitoe's best-known works).

2 What a face can tell you

Look closely/Take/Have a close look at the pictures of Beethoven and the Princess of Wales. **Are** they **like each other?** Hardly, but they have one thing in common: both are 'left-faced'. According to a new theory, which the American professor Karl Smith has published/presented/announced to the public after 15 years of research, each (one) of us is either 'left-faced' or 'right-faced'. With 'left-facers'/In the case of 'left-facers', the muscles on the left side of the face **develop** more

22 Reflexive and Reciprocal Pronouns

strongly/are more strongly developed, and the left eyebrow is mostly/usually higher. These characteristics **are linked** with the ability to use the right side (the 'musical' side) of the brain particularly intensively. Smith has discovered that nearly all musically gifted/talented people are in fact/indeed 'left-facers'. Photographs and portraits of famous musicians confirm this (theory)/This **can be confirmed** by ...

But only about 10–15% of the population are 'left-facers'. For this reason/So Smith advises all parents that **are wondering** whether to pay for expensive music lessons for their child: 'First **look at** your child critically, to check/to see/to find out whether the lessons will **be worthwhile**.' So with the help of this simple 'test'/By using this simple 'test', members of the family and friends who **have known each other** for years can now **get to know each other** from a completely new angle!

The many 'right-facers' among us should not **worry**, however. For Smith has discovered that nearly all leading politicians, mathematicians, actors and athletes are 'right-faced'. Especially dancers and athletes **rely on** a highly developed understanding of movement, which 'right-facers' get by intensive use of the left side of the brain. No wonder then that all the athletes who **competed against each other** at the Olympic Games in Seoul were 'right-facers'. **Test yourself! Look at yourself** in the mirror. Which group do you belong to?